Rhymes and Rhythm

A poem-based course
for English pronunciation

Garnet
EDUCATION

Michael Vaughan-Rees

Published by
Garnet Publishing Ltd.
8 Southern Court
South Street
Reading RG1 4QS, UK

First published by Macmillan Publishers Ltd. 1994.

This edition first published 2010.

ISBN: 978 1 85964 528 4

British Cataloguing-in-Publication Data
A catalogue record for this book is available from the British Library.

Production
Project manager: Toynbee Editorial Services Ltd
Editorial team: Kate Brown, Jo Caulkett, Vale Dominguez
Design: Bookcraft Ltd
Typesetting: Allset Journals & Books, Scarborough, UK
Illustration: Doug Nash
Audio production: Matinée Sound and Vision

Every effort has been made to trace the copyright holders and we apologize in advance for
any unintentional omissions. We will be happy to insert the appropriate acknowledgements
in any subsequent editions.

Printed and bound in Lebanon by International Press: interpress@int-press.com

Contents

Dedication

For my wife, Jane Waller, with love and gratitude.

Jane is happy to share this dedication with my cousin Justin Rees. Justin, a fine, gentle man and talented musician, wrote the backing tracks for the original edition. And when I told him that I needed extra material for this edition he immediately started coming up with ideas. Sadly, before putting any of it down, he died suddenly, at the age of 40, and is much missed by family and friends.

General introduction

This book uses a variety of different types of poem to make it easier for the learner of English to understand spoken English and also to be better understood by native speakers of English. The poems range from very traditional forms, the **limerick**, for example, to contemporary forms such as the **rap**. But whatever the type of poem, they have something in common: they all **rhyme**, and they all have a regular **metre** (that is to say, a regular **beat** or **rhythm**).

This means two things: first, they are easy to repeat and remember; second, they can follow the natural rhythm of spoken English. This second point is very important, since English – unlike many languages – depends on a fairly regular beat going from stressed syllable to stressed syllable. You have to make sure you stress the correct syllables, since mistakes of stress are one of the main reasons why a person may be difficult to understand.

The main beats in the poems in this book always correspond to the stressed syllables. This means that if you keep to the beat, then you automatically stress the correct syllables. Take the beginning of two of the poems, each with the same ONE two three, ONE two three beat:

1   **Nor**man's from **Not**tingham, **Mar**tin's from **Mot**tingham,
    Charley's from **Ches**ter and **Les**ley's from **Lee**;
    Joyce is from **Jar**row and **Hen**ry's from **Har**row,
    Laura's from **Lei**cester and **Dave's** from Dun**dee**.

2   **Ti**na's a **tea**cher, Pris**cil**la's a **prea**cher,
    Donald's a **doc**tor and **Ted** drives a **truck**.
    Fred's a pho**tog**rapher, **Joe's** a ge**og**rapher;
    Barry's a **bar**rister **down** on his **luck**.

The main beat (the ONE of the ONE two three) is marked in **bold**. Keep to that beat and you will soon become aware that the majority of two-syllable nouns are stressed on the first syllable. Not only that: you are forced, for example, to realize that *Leicester* has only two syllables (like *Laura, Charley, teacher, doctor*), that *Dundee* (unusually) has the stress on the second syllable, and that *photographer* and *geographer* have the main stress on the second syllable. And the regular rhyme scheme tells you, for instance, that *Leicester* rhymes with *Chester*.

Now look at another extract:

1   **Per**cy per**suad**ed the **troops** to sur**ren**der
    Betty be**came** a quite **fa**mous ce**leb**rity
    Colin col**lec**ted some **mar**vellous **fur**niture
    Avril a**ver**ted a **ma**jor ca**tas**trophe

This time, the beat forces you to stress the verbs, correctly, on the **second** syllable. And if you keep to the original speed you must, again correctly, make the first syllable of each verb very, very short.

You can come in at any point in the book. But there is a logic to the way it is laid out. Parts I and II concentrate on the main things that speakers may choose to do if they wish to sound more like native speakers: correct syllable length; linking; weak and strong forms; short and long vowels; rules for placement of stress. And if you want people to understand you better, then you should make sure you try to stress the correct syllables.

(Note, however, that you do not have to shorten weak syllables as much as native speakers do, unless you want to speak as fast as we do.)

Part III looks at what really happens in fast, natural speech, so this is where your ears will be trained in order to understand spoken English better (and where you will become aware of how to sound more natural, if that is your aim). Part IV contains a number of poems to help you practise what has been covered earlier, as well as providing a range of vocabulary work.

Vocabulary (and grammar) work is, in fact, built into the course throughout. And many of the tasks rely on skill in understanding the words as well as the sounds and rhythm. But do not feel that you have to understand every word of a poem before you can start to listen to or repeat it. Before you even look at the vocabulary explanations, just listen to a given poem many, many times. Let the words flow over you. Concentrate not just on the **rhythm** of the language, but also on the **music**, the way the words flow up and down (the **intonation**, in fact). When I learn a new language, I imagine the sentences swimming by like great fish in the sea. I see them going up and down (and English goes up and down in a great way, in long flowing movements). So listen and listen first. Then take the book and listen again while reading to yourself. Next, listen to short sections, stop the recording and repeat. Listen, stop and repeat. Finally, you will be able to read along with the recordings, as if you were swimming along to the rhythm and music of English.

There are several icons in the margins to help you make the most of the book:

 These icons give you the corresponding recording number on the accompanying audio CD, making it easy to find the correct one.

 These icons give a quick indication of a poem's level of difficulty on a scale 1 (simplest) to 5 (complex).

 These icons flag up supporting material in the teacher notes on the CD-ROM.

Also, look out for the tasks I've set you (**Task 1**, **Task 2**, ...), these will challenge you to use the information and skills you have just learnt, reinforcing them through practice.

Above all, enjoy yourselves. Have fun. That's what it's all about.

Michael Vaughan-Rees
London, 2010

PART I Syllables, stress and rhythm

As I said in the Introduction, the use of very rhythmic poems will help learners of English to sound more natural when they speak. Most importantly, if you hit the beat correctly you will give correct importance to the most important syllables.

Or, as I say later:

If you don't want your English to sound a mess,
You've got to hit the beat, you've got to hit the stress.
But it's going to sound funny, it's going to go wrong
If you make your weak sounds much too strong.

In this first Part, you will hear a lot about the most common vowel sound in English, the schwa. Now do not worry if you do not make this sound as short and weak as most native speakers do. Unless you want people to think you are British, or any other type of native speaker, you do not have to sound like us. (When I first started teaching English as a Foreign Language, I thought that my job was to help people sound as much like me as possible. But that was long ago and opinions have changed a great deal since then.)

What I think *is* important is to make the stressed syllables definitely longer than the very weak ones. Native speakers, I am certain, find it difficult to understand speakers who get the stresses in the wrong place. (Speakers whose first language is not English may not have such problems, since they usually do not try to speak as fast as we do.)

The most important thing to do with the poems is to enjoy them. As I said earlier, listen to them many times, letting the sounds flow over you. And I hope that you like the backing tracks, which many of the poems have. If you like the idea of making your own backing tracks (for your own language, if you wish) you can get hold of an Apple computer and use the Garage Band application. That's what I have done for this edition, with help from my friend Jon Starling. There are hundreds of different rhythmic loops (percussion, bass, guitar, etc.), going from hip hop to jazz, Indian tabla to Middle Eastern sarod. And it's all free to use, and so easy even I can use it. Just drag and drop.

Chapter 1
Syllables, stress and rhythm

How many syllables?

> All words consist of one or more **syllables**. In that first sentence, for example, the words *all, words, of, one, or* and *more* just have one syllable, *consist* has two, and *syllables* has three.

Listen to the following words. The number of syllables is given at the beginning of each group.

(one)   Jane / house / blue / Spain / pears / grow / work / watch / watched / loud / hunt / give

(two)   Susan / houses / yellow / Japan / apples / grower / working / watchful / aloud / hunted / decide / forgive / photo

(three) Timothy / indigo / Germany / bananas / workable / workmanship / watchfulness / decisive / decided / forgiven / tomorrow / cigarette / photograph

(four)   Elizabeth / indecisive / Argentina / pomegranates / unforgiven / unworkable / photography / photographic

Task 1   Decide how many syllables there are in each of the following words.

biology ( )	bridge ( )	strength ( )	photographer ( )
watches ( )	unabridged ( )	support ( )	jumped ( )
jumpers ( )	policeman ( )	decided ( )	obeyed ( )

The importance of stress

> It is important to become aware of the number of syllables in a word. But if you want to speak English with the correct rhythm, there is something even more important: the place of **stress**.

Listen to the following sequence:

■   ■   ■

Jane, Susan and Timothy.

The first name has one syllable, the second has two and the last has three. But only one syllable in each word is heavily **stressed**. You can see this more clearly if we change the size of the written syllables, according to their relative importance. So, imagine them as:

■   ■ ○   ■ ○ ○

Jane, Susan and Timothy

Stressed syllables, such as Jane, Su and Ti, are different from **unstressed** (sometimes called **weak**) syllables in a number of ways. To start with, they tend to be both relatively **loud** and **long**; relative, that is not only to any other syllables in the same word but also to unimportant words such as *and*.

The importance of stressed syllables in terms of rhythm can be shown if we change the order of the sequence of names.

Listen to the following names. Then repeat each line, keeping to the same rhythm. Clap your hands, click your fingers or tap on the desk to keep to the beat.

■　　■　　　■　　　　　　■　　■　　　■

Jane, Susan and Timothy.　　　　Timothy, Susan and Jane.

Susan, Jane and Timothy.　　　　Jane, Timothy and Susan.

Timothy, Jane and Susan.　　　　Susan, Timothy and Jane.

■　　■　　　■　　pause　　■　　■　　　■　　pause

　　recording　　　　　　　　　　you

Jane, Susan and Timothy.　　　　(Jane, Susan and Timothy)

Susan, Jane and Timothy.　　　　(Susan, Jane and Timothy)

Timothy, Jane and Susan.　　　　(Timothy, Jane and Susan)

Timothy, Susan and Jane.　　　　(Timothy, Susan and Jane)

Jane, Timothy and Susan.　　　　(Jane, Timothy and Susan)

Susan, Timothy and Jane.　　　　(Susan, Timothy and Jane)

It doesn't matter that the three names have different numbers of syllables. And it doesn't matter in which order they are said. The time between the stressed syllables remains more or less the same, which means that the beat stays the same.

But we can only keep to the ONE TWO THREE beat if we make sure that:

a) the stressed syllable is louder and longer than the others;

b) the weak syllables are really weak.

Task 2 **Complete the table using the words below according to the number of syllables.**

Ann / elephant / Volga / Felicity / Spain / Wolverhampton / Nile / rhinoceros / Alexander / Jemima / Japan / Amazon / bear / George / Cardiff / Janet / Peter / Afghanistan / giraffe / Leith / Mississippi / Anthony / Manchester / Morocco

	1 syllable	2 syllables	3 syllables	4 syllables
Cities	Leith	Cardiff	Manchester	Wolverhampton
Boys' names				
Girls' names				
Animals				
Countries				
Rivers				

Where is the stress?

Listen to the following two-syllable words.

Janet / Japan / Volga / giraffe / Cardiff / Peter

Each of them has, of course, one **stressed** syllable and one **weak** syllable. But which is which?

Which words have the stress pattern ■ ○ (with the stress on the first syllable)?

And which have the pattern ○ ■ (with the stress on the second)?

Rhymes and Rhythm

Listen to the words once more. Two words start with a weak syllable, the rest with a strong, stressed syllable.

○ ■ girαffe / Jαpan

■ ○ jαnet / vοlga / cαrdiff / pεter

> Do not be surprised that there are more of one pattern than the other; the vast majority of two-syllable nouns (names included) have the stress pattern ■ ○. (As we shall see later, most two-syllable **verbs** are the other way round, having the pattern ○ ■.)
>
> With three-syllable words there are, of course, three possible patterns:
>
> ■ ○ ○ = stress on 1st syllable
>
> ○ ■ ○ = stress on 2nd syllable
>
> ○ ○ ■ = stress on 3rd syllable

Task 3 Listen to the three-syllable words from the list below and complete the table placing them according to their stress pattern.

Manchester / Anthony / Jemima / elephant / Morocco / Amazon

■ ○ ○	○ ■ ○	○ ○ ■

> Yes, there was nothing in the third column. In fact there are very few ○ ○ ■ words of any sort. They tend to be either imports, such as *cigarette* and *chimpanzee*, or words such as *Japanese* and *picturesque*, where the ending is so strong that it becomes the main stress.
>
> Nouns with the ○ ■ ○ pattern are quite rare too, unless they are derived from verbs (*accountant / allowance / believer / enquiry / excitement*, etc.). And many of them, like *Jemima* and *Morocco*, are imports ending in a vowel letter/sound; think about *banana, tobacco, spaghetti*, for example.

Task 4 Now listen to the four-syllable words, and complete the table as before.

Felicity / Afghanistan / Alexander / Wolverhampton / rhinoceros / Mississippi

Only two stress patterns are given, since it is rare for four-syllable words to be stressed on the first or last syllable.

○ ■ ○ ○	○ ○ ■ ○

Primary and secondary stress

Listen again to the four-syllable words. In *Alexander*, *Wolverhampton* and *Mississippi*, those with the ○ ○ ■ ○ pattern, the first syllable sounds stronger than the second and fourth, but not as strong as the third. Think of them as:

Alex**an**der / Wolver**hamp**ton / Missi**ssi**ppi

A similar thing happens in the case of three-syllable words with the ○ ○ ■ pattern, for example:

ciga**rette** / chimpan**zee** / Japa**nese** / pictu**resque**

It is not enough, then, simply to talk of syllables as being either **stressed** or **weak**; with words of three or more syllables it may be necessary to distinguish three degrees of stress:

primary, **secondary** and **weak** (or unstressed)

■   •   ○

So, in the case of these two patterns it might be better to show them as:

● ○ ■ (e.g., *cigarette*) = secondary stress + weak + primary stress, and

● ○ ■ ○ (e.g., *Alexander*) = secondary stress + weak + primary stress + weak[1]

Weak syllables and schwa

As a general rule we can say that every syllable contains a vowel sound.[2] A second general rule is that the shorter the vowel, the shorter and weaker the syllable.

Now let us take another look at some of the words already examined, this time concentrating on the vowel sounds in the weak syllables. To help us do this we will start to use phonetic notation, where one symbol = one sound. This is because standard spelling often makes it difficult to see what the sounds really are.

Janet	■ ○	**Ja**net	/ˈdʒænɪt/ or /ˈdʒænət/
Peter	■ ○	**Pe**ter	/ˈpiːtə/
giraffe	○ ■	gi**raffe**	/dʒəˈrɑːf/
Japan	○ ■	Ja**pan**	/dʒəˈpæn/
elephant	■ ○ ○	**e**lephant	/ˈelɪfənt or /ˈeləfənt/
Anthony	■ ○ ○	**An**thony	/ˈæntəni/
Amazon	■ ○ ○	**A**mazon	/ˈæməzən/
Morocco	○ ■ ○	Mo**ro**cco	/məˈrɒkəʊ/
Jemima	○ ■ ○	Je**mi**ma	/dʒɪˈmaɪmə/ or /dʒəˈmaɪmə/
cigarette	● ○ ■	ciga**rette**	/ˌsɪɡəˈret/
Felicity	○ ■ ○ ○	Fe**li**city	/fəˈlɪsəti/
rhinoceros	○ ■ ○ ○	rhi**no**ceros	/raɪˈnɒsərəs/
Wolverhampton	● ○ ■ ○	Wolver**hamp**ton	/ˌwʊlvəˈhæmptən/
Mississippi	● ○ ■ ○	Missi**ssi**ppi	/ˌmɪsɪˈsɪpi/ or /ˌmɪsəˈsɪpi/

1 The rules of stress cover words in isolation, in their dictionary form. In Part II we will see how stress may shift according to word function.

2 The exception is in such words as *curtain* or *bottle* where /n/ and /l/ may act as 'syllabic consonants', with no need for a preceding short vowel.

Rhymes and Rhythm

If we enlarge the phonetic notation it is easy to see which is the most common vowel sound in the weak, unstressed syllables.

Morocco	/məˈrɒkəʊ/	Amazon	/ˈæməzən/
giraffe	/dʒəˈrɑːf/	Peter	/ˈpiːtə/
Japan	/dʒəˈpæn/	Anthony	/ˈæntəni/
Felicity	/fəˈlɪsəti/	rhinoceros	/raiˈnɒsərəs/
cigarette	/ˌsɪgəˈret/	elephant	/ˈelɪfənt/ or /ˈeləfənt/
Jemima	/dʒɪˈmaɪmə/ or /dʒəˈmaɪmə/	Janet	ˈdʒænɪt or /ˈdʒænət/
Wolverhampton	/ˌwʊlvəˈhæmptən/		

The most common sound by far is the one in blue. This is the vowel represented by the symbol /ə/ and it is the only vowel important enough to be given its own name: **schwa**.

> The schwa (sometimes spelled **shwa**) is not only the most common vowel sound in weak syllables; it is by far the most common vowel sound in the whole of the English system. Look at its distribution in the words above. It is found:
>
> *   at the start of words, just before the main stress:
>   e.g., *Mo*rocco, *Ja*pan, *gi*raffe, *Fe*licity
>
> *   following main stress (sometimes twice in ■ ○ ○ words):
>   e.g., Pe*ter*, Am*azon*, An*tho*ny
>
> *   between secondary and primary stress:
>   e.g., cig*a*rette, Wol*ver*hampton
>
> *   as an even shorter alternative to short /ɪ/ in fast versions of certain words:
>   e.g., Ja*net*, *Je*mima, e*le*phant

Schwa is not just short, it is the shortest possible vowel in English. Listen to how little difference the presence of schwa can make to a word.

Words without schwa	Words with schwa
sport = /spɔːt/	support = /səˈpɔːt/
claps = /klæps/	collapse = /kəˈlæps/
prayed = /preɪd/	parade = /pəˈreɪd/
train = /treɪn/	terrain = /təˈreɪn/
blow = /bləʊ/	below = /bəˈləʊ/
plight = /plaɪt/	polite = /pəˈlaɪt/
Clyde = /klaɪd/	collide = /kəˈlaɪd/
hungry = /ˈhʌngri/	Hungary = /ˈhʌngəri/
Britney = /ˈbrɪtni/	Brittany = /ˈbrɪtəni/

> Note that there is no single written vowel that corresponds to schwa. So there is no point in trying to learn all the possible written forms where the schwa sound can be found.
>
> Note also that schwa is not essential. But do try to make strong syllables more important than weak ones.

Task 5   Listen to the following words, all taken from page 4, and circle the syllables containing schwa. (Note, not all words contain schwa.)

grower	yellow	aloud	hunted	forgive	photo
Timothy	Germany	bananas	workmanship	tomorrow	Elizabeth
Argentina	photograph	photography	photographic		

Stress and rhythm

When we looked at the Jane, Susan and Timothy sequence, we saw that it is possible to keep to a more or less regular beat, based on stressed syllables, provided that:

a) the stressed syllable is louder and longer than the others;

b) the weak syllables are really weak.

You can demonstrate this by using the first line of a famous children's rhyme called 'This is the **house** that **Jack built**'. It has four beats, corresponding to the stressed syllables marked in bold in the previous line. But note that the first beat is followed by two weak syllables, the next by one, then by none. So you have to imagine the rhythm of the line as:

ONE			TWO		THREE	FOUR
■	○	○	■	○	■	■
DAH	du	du	DAH	du	DAH	DAH
This	is	the	house	that	Jack	built

(Note the use of DAH du du DAH du DAH DAH. You can always use these nonsense syllables to get the rhythm of sentences without having to worry about an exact pronunciation. Just remember that DAH is relatively **long and loud** while du is relatively **short and quiet**.)

Task 6   **Listen to what happens if we keep to the same four-beat rhythm, while changing the words and varying the number of weak syllables.**

ONE			TWO			THREE		FOUR
■	○	○	■	○	○	■	○ ○	■
DAH	du	du	DAH	du	du	DAH	du du	DAH
These	are	the	hous	es	that	Ja	queline	built

Now try this longer sequence, still keeping to the same rhythm.

ONE	TWO	THREE	FOUR
This is the	house that	Jack	built
These are the	houses that	Jack	built
These are the	houses that	Jaqueline	built
This is the	house that my	mother	deSigned
This is the	bicycle	Peter	repaired
Those are the	peOple we	met in the	park
That is the	perSon I	saw on the	stairs
Those are the	peOple we	drove to the	party
That is the	garDener who	works for my	mother
Andrew is	taLLer than	Peter and	Thomas
Fancy a	glass of	Italian	brandy?
Tom's not as	tall as the	rest of the	family
What an	amazingly	lively	proDuction!
How can we	possibly	get there in	time!

Schwa in grammatical items

Schwa is found not only in **lexical items** (nouns, main verbs, adjectives and adverbs). It is regularly found in common, weakly-stressed **grammatical items**, especially prepositions, articles, auxiliary verbs and pronouns.

Listen again to the 'This house that Jack built' sequence and see if you can spot the grammatical items containing schwa.

Strong and weak forms of grammatical items

In the previous task we concentrated on weakly stressed grammatical items, all containing schwa. But be careful; do not assume that such items always contain schwa.

This can depend on:

*   what the item is doing (i.e., its **function**) and/or;

*   where the item is found (i.e., its **position**).

The word *that*, for example, has two different functions.

1   In 'This is the house **that** Jack built' it is a weakly stressed relative pronoun, with schwa. /ðət/

2   In '**That** is the gardener who works for my mother' it is a strongly stressed demonstrative pronoun, with a different, stronger vowel. /ðæt/

The definite article *the* has two different pronunciations according to the following sound.

1   When the next word begins with a consonant (e.g., *the house / the people*) it is the weak form with schwa: /ðə ˈhaʊs/ or /ðə ˈpiːpəl/.

2   But when followed by a vowel (as in *the old man*) it is pronounced /ði/, with a /j/ sound linking it to the vowel /ði ʲˈəʊld mæn/.[3]

The preposition *to* changes according to the following sound and its position in the sentence.

1   When followed by a consonant (e.g., *to the party*), the weak form with schwa is used: /tə ðə ˈpɑːti/.

2   When followed by a vowel (as in *to a party*), it contains a stronger vowel with a /w/ sound linking it to the vowel: /tu ʷə ˈpɑːti/.

3   Finally, if *to* ends a sequence (e.g., *That's where I'm going to*), it is pronounced /tuː/ with an even stronger, longer vowel, as if it were *too* or *two*.

We can say the same about a number of other grammatical items, notably: the **pronouns** he, her, him and them; the **possessive adjectives** her and his; and **modal** and **auxiliary** verbs. These, too, have various **strong** and **weak** forms, and the strongest form of all is used in contrast with another word.

Take the **pronouns** and possessive **adjectives**. Compare.

strong forms (associated with pointing and/or contrast)

1   **He** is the one who did it!   (/ˈhiː ʲɪz ðə wʌn/ ...)

2   I gave it to **him** not **her**!   (... /tʊ ˈhɪm nɒt ˈhɜː/)

3   It was **them** I saw, over **there**!   (... /ˈðem/ ... /ˈðeə/)

4   It was **her** fault, not **his**!   (... /ˈhɜː/ ... /ˈhɪz/)

5   **We** did it, not **you**!   (/ˈwiː/ ... /ˈjuː/)

---

3   The article *the* also has the form /ðiː/ when heavily stressed, as in the following exchange: '*My father met Michael Jackson once.' 'The Michael Jackson?*'

very weak forms (usually found after a stressed verb)

1   Where's Peter?
    I **think** he's over **there**.   /aɪ ˈθɪŋk iz/

2   Where's Jane?
    I've just **left** her on her **own**.   /ˈdʒʌs ˈleft ə rɒn ə ˈrəʊn/

3   Where's John?
    I've just **left** him on his **own**.   /dʒʌs ˈleft ɪm ɒnɪ ˈzəʊn/

4   Where are your parents?
    I've just **left** them on their **own**.   /ˈdʒʌs ˈleft əm ɒn ðə ˈrəʊn/)

5   She's always **play**ing her gui**tar**.   /ˈpleɪ ʲɪŋ ə gɪˈtɑː/

> Note that more than one weak form may be possible: for example, *her* can be /hə/ or /ə/; *them* can be /ðəm/ or /əm/; *you* can be /ju/ or /jə/. Note, too, that the very weak forms of *her*, *him* and *them* can involve not only a weakening of the vowel, but also **elision** of the consonant at the start of the word. This will be looked at in greater detail in Part 3.

Rhythm and linking

> In the previous section, the word **linking** was used for the first time. So far, you have learned that in order to keep to the rhythm you have to hit the stressed syllables and weaken the weak syllables. But there is one more important factor: the rhythm can only flow if words are properly **linked**.
>
> I use the word 'flow' because it can help to think of words as a stream, with no division between them. Or you may prefer to imagine the words as a chain, all joined (or **linked**) together.

There are four main ways of linking words. Here is a simple sequence to help you remember them.

One apple, two apples, three apples, four apples

In each case, the number links smoothly to the following vowel sound, so that the next word sounds as if it doesn't start with a vowel at all. Imagine it like this:

	written as	sounds like	phonetic notation
1	One apple	wu napple	/wʌ næpəl/
2	Two apples	two wapples	/tuː ʷæpəlz/
3	Three apples	three yapples	/θriː ʲæpəlz/
4	Four apples	four rapples	/fɔː ræpəlz/

Now let's look at these four types of linking in greater detail.

Consonant to vowel *one apple*

> When a word ending in a consonant is followed by a word beginning with a vowel, there is a smooth link. If the word beginning with the vowel is stressed, then the moment of stress seems to begin with the preceding consonant. Compare the following sequences, which sound exactly the same.

a)   What we need is a name.   /əˈneɪm/

b)   What we need is an aim.   /əˈneɪm/

This is the most common form of linking, and there were several examples in the 'This is the house that Jack built' sequence, including:

a glass_of_Italian brandy

Tom's not_as tall_as the rest_of the family.

That_is the person_I saw on the stairs.

Rounded vowel to vowel *two apples*

> Where a word ends with one of the rounded vowels /əʊ/, /aʊ/, /uː/ (as in *so, now, too*) there is a /w/ link.

For example:

so (h)e's left! =   /səʊ ʷiːz 'left/

too old =   /tʊː ʷəʊld/

Andrew is taller =   /'ændruː ʷɪz 'tɔːlə/

This is presumably due to the fact that the lips are coming together anyway, and the consequent parting of the lips in preparation for the next vowel forces a /w/.

Spread/stretched vowel to vowel *three apples*

> When a word ends with /iː/ (as in *see, he, she*) or one of the diphthongs of which /ɪ/ is the second element (/aɪ/, /eɪ/, /ɔɪ/, as in *my, they, boy*) there is an off-glide to /j/.

For example:

yes, I am =   /je saɪ ʲæm/   Fancy a glass? =   /'fænsi ʲə 'glɑːs/

very often =   /veri ʲɒfən/   my uncle =   /maɪ ʲʌŋkəl/

/r/ to vowel *four apples*

> In many dialects of English (including General American and several found in Britain), the written *r* in words such as *mother, for* and *far* has a corresponding /r/ sound. But in RP, an /r/ sound is only heard when there is a following vowel.

Compare the following:

far =   /fɑː/   far away =   /fɑːrə 'weɪ/

for weeks =   /fə 'wiːks/   for ever =   /fə 'revə/

mother =   /'mʌðə/   mother-in-law =   /'mʌðərɪn 'lɔː/

Peter =   /'piːtə/   Peter and Tom =   /'piːtərən 'tɒm/

> ***Two other forms of linking***
> There are two other types of link which you should know about. Don't feel that you have to imitate them, but you will be able to understand spoken English more easily if you are aware of them.

'Intrusive' /r/ to vowel

> In many words ending with the written consonant *r* the final vowel sound is one of the following: schwa (teacher / harbour / actor / etc.); /ɔː/ (four / door / pour / etc.) and /ɑː/ (car / far / bar / etc.). No doubt as a result of this, there is a tendency to insert a linking /r/ when a word ends in one of these vowel sounds, even when no written *r* exists.

For example:

America and Asia =   /ə'merɪkə rə 'neɪʒə/

Asia and America =   /'eɪʒə rə nə 'merɪkə/

law and order =   /ˌlɔː rə 'nɔːdə/

Shah of Persia =   /ʃɑː rəv 'pɜːʃə/ or /'pɜːʒə/

Careful with this one. Many people consider that 'intrusive' /r/ is sub-standard, and certainly not to be imitated.

Consonant to consonant linking

Many words in English start with clusters of two or three consonant sounds. For example, *play / splay / train / strain / dry / try / fly*, and so on.

So when a word ending in a consonant sound is followed by a word beginning with another consonant **with which it can form a cluster**, then there is a tendency for that cluster to occur.

That sounds rather complicated, but is actually a description of what happens with, for example, *cold rain*, where the /d/ is drawn towards the /r/ (since the initial cluster /dr/ is highly productive) so that it sounds like *coal drain*, with the stress starting on /dr/ and not on /r/. Other examples include:

actual words	sounds like	phonetic notation
ice cream	I scream	/aɪ ˈskriːm/
next week	necks tweak	/ˌneks ˈtwiːk/
six trains	sick strains	/ˌsɪk ˈstreɪnz/
might rise	my tries	/ˌmaɪ ˈtraɪz
Regent's Park	region spark	/ˌriːdʒən(t) ˈspɑːk/

Billy yate a napple, a nice ri papple

Below, there is a chant to help you practise the first three types of linking. The chant is written with the correct spelling on the left of the page, but you actually say it the way it is written on the right.

Vocabulary notes

Apples, oranges and *apricots* are fruit; *onions, artichokes* and *aubergines* are vegetables; *almonds* are nuts; *eels* look like snakes, but live in rivers or the sea; *oysters* are shell-fish which you cut open and eat with a little lemon-juice; *crunchy* here is the opposite of *soft*; *runny* means not cooked for long; you can *smoke* different types of fish, salmon, for example.

How it's written	How it sounds
Billy ate an apple, a nice ripe apple	Billy yate a napple, a nice ri papple
Beattie ate an orange, a nice juicy orange	Beattie yate a norange, a nice juicy yorange
Lucy ate an ice cream, a nice creamy ice cream	Lucy yate a ni scream, a nigh screamy yi scream
Flo ate an apricot, a nice yellow apricot	Flo wate a napricot, a nice yellow wapricot
Mo ate an omelette, a nice runny omelette	Mo wate a nomélette, a nice runny yomelette
Chloe ate an egg, a nice brown egg	Chloe yate a negg, a nice brow negg
Nelly ate an almond, a nice crunchy almond	Nelly yate a nalmond, a nigh scrunchy yalmond
Sally ate an onion, a nice Spanish onion	Sally yate a nonion, a nigh Spani shonion
Alex ate an artichoke, a nice tasty artichoke	Alec sate a nartichoke, a nigh stasty yartichoke
Andrew ate an aubergine, a nice spicy aubergine	Andrew wate a naubergine, a nigh spicy yaubergine
Mary ate an olive a nice Greek olive	Mary yate a nolive, a nigh scree colive
Carol ate an eel, a nice smoked eel	Caro late a neel, a nigh smoke teel
Alice ate an oyster, a nice fresh oyster	Alice sate a noyster, a nice fre shoyster

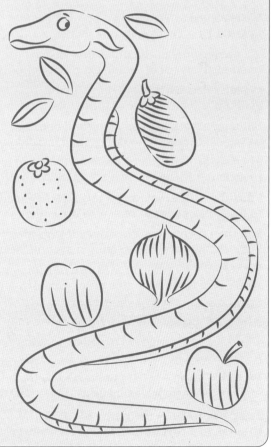

And what kind of summer did you have?

Here is a chance for you to practise what we've been looking at so far. The poem below has a simple, driving **ONE two three ONE two three** beat. But you will only keep to the beat if you remember to:

1   hit the main stressed syllables (shown **in bold** in the first three verses);

2   watch out for the weak syllables in the names; a lot of them start with an unstressed syllable containing schwa;

3   watch out also for the weak forms of short grammatical words such as *to*, *and*, *that* and *of*;

4   make the links between words where necessary;

5   and don't be afraid to leave out (**elide**) the occasional sound. We'll be looking at this in greater detail in Part 3, but for the moment just note that *and* often loses its final /d/, especially when followed by a consonant; and *of* may lose its /v/ and become schwa, also when followed by a consonant. All of these things happen in the second verse, as you can see when it is written in phonetic notation.

■	■	■	■
/wɪ 'drəʊv θruː ðə	'naɪt tʊ ᵂɜ	'vɪlɪdʒ nɪə	'brʌsəlz/
/tə 'tʃuz lɒtsə	'buːz ən iː(t)	'plɛnti ʲə	'mʌsəlz/

> **Vocabulary notes**
> *booze (noun/verb)* is slang for '(alcoholic) drink';
> to *falter* is to stop doing something smoothly; talking for instance;
> a *Fiesta* is a type of Ford car;
> *gear* is a general word for 'things';
> a *fee* is money paid for professional services (to a lawyer, architect, etc.);
> a *loner* is a person who prefers to be alone;
> *mussels* are shellfish which are very popular in Belgium;
> *replenish* is a formal verb meaning 'fill'.

3/4

We **tra**velled to **Ve**nice then on to Ve**ro**na
to **test** a Fi**es**ta with **on**ly one **own**er.

We **drove** through the **night** to a **vil**lage near **Bru**ssels
to **choose** lots of **booze** and eat **plen**ty of **mus**sels.

We **la**ter de**ci**ded to **head** off to **Spain**
via **France** for a **chance** to drink **lots** of cham**pagne**.

But after a week of good living and booze
we agreed that we'd need to rest up in Toulouse.

Then we drove to Madrid before heading to Lisbon
to meet our friend Pete who'd just flown in from Brisbane.

We drove farther south to a town near Granada
to find lots of wine to replenish the larder,

and then spent a week just outside Algeciras,
but folk that we spoke to refused to come near us.

We stayed for a while in the town of Pamplona
where Pete walked the street (he's a bit of a loner).

We drove fairly fast to a hotel in Cannes
where we tried to confide our affairs to a man,

who gave us some goods to deliver in Rome
for a fee we'd not see until safely back home.

We sailed down to Malta to stay in Valetta
but a fax sent from Sfax made us think that we'd better

cross over to Tunis then drive to Algiers
to speak to a Greek I had known for some years.

We drove through Morocco to reach Casablanca
to discuss, without fuss, our affairs with a banker.

Then headed back north, crossed the Straits of Gibraltar
but passed through so fast we were starting to falter,

and round about then I began to remember
I had to meet Dad on the tenth of September.

We sold the Fiesta and loaded a plane
then with some gear from Tangier then we got on a train,

which roared through the night till it reached Santander
where we stayed one more day just to breathe in the air,

then a boat brought us back to our own native shores.
So that was my holiday, how about yours?

Task 7   Your task is:

a) to write the place names in the table according to their stress pattern (two have been done as examples);

b) to find the odd one out; that is to say, the name which follows a pattern not represented in the grid.

■	○■	■○	○■○	●○■○
	Madrid		Valetta	

Rhymes, rhythm and alliteration

The remaining practice poems in Part I include one extra element, **alliteration**; that is to say, the repetition of initial consonant sounds at the start of words.

Names

In the first poem, 'Names from the British Isles', each line contains an English first name, followed by a British place name, both starting with the same sound (usually a consonant, but there are two examples of vowels being repeated).

As with the previous poem – 'What kind of summer did you have?' – this has a simple **ONE two three ONE two three** waltz beat. But you can only keep to the beat if you remember the following:

1 Several common place name endings have become so weak that the vowels have been reduced to schwa.

~ham = /əm/	Nottingham = /ˈnɒtɪŋəm/	Birmingham = /ˈbɜːmɪŋəm/
~ster = /stə/	Leicester = /ˈlestə/	Gloucester = /ˈglɒstə/
~ton = /tən/	Paignton = /ˈpeɪntən/	Taunton = /ˈtɔːntən/
~ford = /fəd/	Stratford = /ˈstrætfəd/	Oxford = /ˈɒksfəd/

2 Most two-syllable nouns start with a stressed syllable and end with a weaker syllable (often containing schwa). Place names are no exception. But watch out for those that have the main stress on the second syllable, for example:

Dundee   Kildare   Argyll /ɑːˈgaɪl/   Carlisle /kɑːˈlaɪl/

3 Most two-syllable first names also start with a stressed syllable. But a number of names (especially those ending with ~a) have the main stress two syllables from the end, for example:

Patricia = /pəˈtrɪʃə/   Amanda = /əˈmændə/   Belinda = /bəˈlɪndə/   Theresa = /təˈriːzə/ or /təˈreɪzə/

This happens with place names such as *Reno, Montana* and *Colorado.* (Look at the poem on page 17 for words such as *banana, spaghetti* and *libretto.*)

4 The preposition *from* is found in its weak /frəm/ form throughout. But the pronunciation of *and* depends on what the next sound is. The /d/ is only certain to be heard when followed by a vowel (so *and Anne* = /ˈdæn/). But the /d/ is **elided** in *and Stan,* for example, and we hear /ən ˈstæn/.

5 Sometimes when the /d/ disappears it allows **assimilation** to take place. This means that a sound changes to be more like the following sound. In *and Patricia,* for example the /d/ goes and then the /n/ becomes /m/ because of the following /p/ and we end up with /əm pəˈtrɪʃə/. In the same way, *and Kate* = /əŋ ˈkeɪt/. (The symbol /ŋ/ represents the consonant sound at the end of *song, thing, wrong,* etc.)

(Don't worry if this is not very clear at the moment. We will look at elision and assimilation in more detail in Part III.)

6 And be careful with the links in, for example, *and_Anne, Chester_and, Joyce_is, from_Argyll,* etc.

Names from the British Isles

1 **Norman**'s from **Nottingham**,
Martin's from **Mottingham**,
Charley's from **Chester**
and **Lesley**'s from **Lee**;
Joyce is from **Jarrow**
and **Henry**'s from **Harrow**,
Laura's from **Leicester**
and **Dave**'s from **Dundee**.

2 **Ted** comes from **Taunton**
and **Stan** comes from **Staunton**
Billy's from **Bolton**
And **Willy**'s from **Ware**;
Mary's from **Marlow**,
and **Harry**'s from **Harlow**
Mike's from South **Molton**
and **Kate**'s from Kil**dare**.

3 **Ken**'s from Car**lisle**
and **Anne**'s from Ar**gyll**,
Fanny's from **Fawley**
and **Harriet**'s from **Hull**;
Teddy's from **Tenby**
and **Den** is from **Den**bigh,
Chris comes from **Crawley**
and **Millie**'s from **Mull**.

4 **Ed** comes from **Eltham**
and **Fred** comes from **Feltham**,
Brian's from **Braintree**
and **Chris** comes from **Crewe**;
Colin's from **Kerry**
and **Bobby**'s from **Bury**,
Ada's from **Aintree**
So, **how** about **you**?

Names from the Americas

1 **Mo**'s from Mon**tana**
and **Sal**'s from Sa**vannah**,
Dave's from Day**tona**
and **Mary**'s from **Maine**;
Nell's from Ne**bra**ska
and **Al**'s from A**laska**,
Will's from Wi**nona**
and **Fred**'s from Fort **Wayne**.

2 **Rick** comes from **Reno**
and **Chick** comes from **Chino**,
Brian's from **Brampton**
and **Rita**'s from **Rome**;
Al's from A**ruba**
and **Connie**'s from **Cuba**
Ned's from North **Hampton**
and **Nora**'s from **Nome**.

3 **Hank**'s from Ha**vana**
and **Guy**'s from Gu**yana**,
Beth comes from **Benton**
and **Nick**'s from North **Bay**;
Charley's from **Chile**
and **Phil** comes from **Philly**,
Trudy's from **Trenton**
and **Luke**'s from LA.

Where do you think you're going?

This is another poem in 3/4 time. The beat is strictly as follows:

and	ONE	2	3	ONE	2	3	ONE	2	3	ONE	2	(and)
du	DAH	du	du	DAH	du	du	DAH	du	du	DAH	du	
I'm	go	ing	to	Leeds	to	lo	cate	a	lib	re	tto	
I'm	go	ing	to	Stock	holm	to	steal	a	sti	le	tto	

16

It is important to remember the following:

1   The place names are either monosyllables (*Leeds, Slough, Cork, Cowes,* etc.) or have the stress pattern ■ ○, as is normal for two-syllable nouns (*Brighton, Ventnor, Poland,* etc.).

2   The verbs are either monosyllables (*buy, view, sell, pinch,* etc.) or have the stress pattern ○ ■, as is normal for two-syllable verbs (*provide, supply, collect, locate, promote, consult, reform, confuse, become*).

3   All the three-syllable nouns at the end of lines have the pattern ○ ■ ○. This is either because they derive from ○ ■ verbs (*professor, confessor, relation, computer, commuter*) or because they are loan words from other languages all ending in a vowel sound (*banana, pyjama, vanilla, confetti, spaghetti, libretto, stiletto, baloney*).

4   The two loan words with four syllables (*sarsparilla* and *macaroni*) have the pattern ● ○ ■ ○, i.e., there is secondary stress on the first syllable and primary stress on the third.

5   If the place has only one syllable (*Leeds, Perth, Cork,* etc.) then the verb has two syllables (*provide, supply, collect*). But if the place has two syllables (*Stockholm, Soho, Poland, Basel*) then the verb has one (*buy, steal, pinch*).

Vocabulary notes
baloney is a type of sausage (from Bologna in Italy);
a *commuter* lives in the suburbs and travels (or commutes) into the city to work;
confetti are bits of coloured paper thrown over the couple after a wedding;
a *libretto* is the words of an opera;
pastrami is a type of smoked beef (US);
pinch is a colloquial word for steal;
sarsparilla is a soft drink made from the sarsparilla plant;
a *steeple* is the tower of a church;
a *stiletto* is a sharp, pointed knife;
vanilla comes from a type of bean and is used for flavouring desserts.

Now listen to the poem very carefully and answer the questions on the next page.

Where do you think you're going?

I'm going to Brighton to buy some bananas
I'm going to Perth to provide some pyjamas

I'm going to Ventnor to view some vanilla
I'm going to Slough to supply sarsparilla

I'm going to Soho to sell some salami
I'm going to Poland to pinch some pastrami

I'm going to Cork to collect some confetti
I'm going to Spain to secure some spaghetti

I'm going to Leeds to locate a libretto
I'm going to Stockholm to steal a stiletto

I'm going to Prague to promote my professor
I'm going to Crewe to consult my confessor

I'm going to Rye to reform a relation
I'm going to Stansted to stare at the station

I'm going to Basel to boil some baloney
I'm going to Minsk for some mixed macaroni

I'm going to Plymouth to please all the people
I'm going to Stockport to stand on the steeple

I'm going to Cowes to confuse a computer
I'm moving to Kent to become a commuter

GREEK ST. W1
SALAMI

Task 8   Which of the two-syllable place names have schwa in the final syllable? Which may have schwa? And which definitely do not have schwa?

Task 9   Which of the final words in each line have schwa in the first syllable?

Task 10   Which of the final words also have schwa in the last syllable?

Task 11   Which of the verbs have schwa in the first syllable?

The do-it-yourself tongue-twister kit

> Every language has what are called **tongue-twisters**: sequences with so many examples of alliteration that even native speakers have problems saying them fast. (Examples in English include: *Peter Piper picked a peck of pickled pepper* and *She sells seashells on the seashore*.)

In 'Names from the British Isles' there were just **two** examples of each consonant sound; *Martin's from Mottingham*, for example. In 'Where do you think you're going?' it went up to **three**; *I'm going to Brighton to buy some bananas*, and so on. In this section, we will end up with five or sometimes six. But we'll make it easier for you by starting with just two examples of the same sound, then building up to three, four, and so on. (It's called 'The do-it-yourself tongue-twister kit' because you start off easy and take your time working up to the more difficult ones.)

Two-part alliteration

The most important syllables in this part are found in the **name** and in what the person **buys** to eat or drink. The word *bought* is more important than the very weak *some* (= /səm/), but it is less important than the main syllables, because it is repeated. Watch out for the words (including names) with stress on the second syllables:

poˈtatoes, baˈnanas, toˈmatoes, Saˈlome, Caˈmilla, Paˈtricia

They all have schwa in the first weak syllable!

> **Vocabulary notes**
> *cabbages* and *potatoes* are vegetables; *peaches* and *bananas* are fruit; *doughnuts*, *chocolate* and *fritters* contain sugar; *cod* is a fish, and *salami* is a type of sausage.

■	•	■
Kenneth	bought some	**cabb**age.
Polly	bought some	**peach**es.
Sally	bought some	salad.
Dennis	bought some	**dough**nuts.
Charles	bought some	**choc**olate.
Shirley	bought some	sugar.
Freddy	bought some	fritters.
Camilla	bought some	**cod.**
Tina	bought some	tomatoes.
Barbara	bought some	bananas.
Salome	bought some	salami
Patricia	bought some	potatoes.

Three-part alliteration

Now we add another word to say how much food or drink is bought. This can be a **container** (*a packet, tin, crate*, etc.); a **quantity** (*a dozen, slice, pound, kilo*, etc.); or we can add *~ful* to some of the nouns. The main syllable in the new word is stressed, but the linking word *of* is very, very weak. When followed by a vowel, we usually pronounce it /əv/, but when followed by a consonant, it often reduces to schwa. This means that *a kilo of cabbage* sounds like *a kilo a cabbage* and *a bunch of bananas* sounds like *a bunch a bananas*.

■	•	■	■
Kenneth	bought a	**kil**o of	**cab**bage.
Polly	bought a	**pack**et of	**peach**es.
Sally	bought a	**sack**ful of	**sal**ad.
Dennis	bought a	**doz**en	**dough**nuts.
Charles	bought a	**chunk** of	**choc**olate.
Shirley	bought a	**shop**ful of	**sug**ar.
Freddy	bought a	**fridge**ful of	**frit**ters.
Camilla	bought a	**crate** of	**cod.**
Tina	bought a	**tin** of	to**ma**toes.
Barbara	bought a	**bunch** of	ba**nan**as.
Salome	bought a	**slice** of	sa**lam**i.
Patricia	bought a	**pound** of	po**tat**oes.

Arthur bought an armful of artichokes

Let's practice this three-part alliteration with the following poem. You will get the rhythm if you pause very slightly after *bought* in each line. Be careful though, the following lines contain four examples of the same initial sound:

Jeremy bought a **gi**ant **jar** of **jam**,
Linda bought a **large leg** of **lamb**.
Charlie bought a **chunk** of **cheap cheese**.

To keep to the rhythm in these lines you have to be careful to reduce the word *of* to a simple schwa and link it to the word before it. It has to sound like a *gian(t) jar a jam / a large leg a lamb / a chunk a cheap cheese.*

Vocabulary notes
Important! Don't feel you have to understand every single word before you start listening to the poems. Concentrate on the rhythm and intonation; listen and start repeating; **then** check the meaning, if you need to.

Artichokes, beans, peas and *spinach* are vegetables; *apricots, lemons* and *quinces* are fruit; *bream* and *sardines* are fish; *lamb, mince* and *steak* refer to meat (*mince* is the meat in hamburgers); a *chunk* is a square piece; *doughnuts* are a type of bun cooked in deep fat and covered with sugar; *muesli* is a breakfast cereal; a *mug* is like a cup, but shaped like a cylinder; a *stone* is 14 pounds, about 6 kilos; *toffee* is made with sugar; *thread* is used for sewing clothes, and when you are sewing, you put a *thimble* on your finger to push the needle through.

Arthur bought (pause) an **arm**ful of **ar**tichokes,
Belinda bought (pause) a **bar**relful of **beans**,
Catherine bought (pause) a **kil**o of **cab**bages, and
Sandra bought (pause) a **sack** of **sar**dines.

Harriet bought a **hand**ful of **hand**kerchiefs,
Jeremy bought a **gi**ant **jar** of **jam**,
Lola bought a **li**tre of **lem**on juice, and
Linda bought a **large leg** of **lamb**.

Peter bought a **pock**etful of **pea**nuts,
Queenie bought a **quar**ter pound **quince**,
Shirley bought a **shop** full of **sug**ar lumps, and
Michael bought a **mil**ligram of **mince**.

Salome bought a **slice** of sa**lam**i,
Charlie bought a **chunk** of **cheap cheese**,
Spencer bought a **spoon**ful of **spin**ach, and
Pamela bought a **pack**et full of **peas**.

Philippa bought a **fol**der for her **pho**tographs,
Stephen bought a **stone** of **steak**.
Amos bought an **a**cre of **a**pricots, and
Katie bought a **ki**logram of **cake**,

Cuthbert bought a **cup**ful of **cus**tard,
Brenda bought a **buck**etful of **bream**,
Matilda bought a **mug**ful of **mus**tard, and
Christopher bought a **crate**ful of **cream**.

Kenneth bought a **car**ton of **coffee**,
Benedict bought a **bas**ket full of **bread**,
Tina bought a **tin**ful of **toffee**, and
Theo bought a **thim**ble full of **thread**.

Brian bought some **bread** for his **bro**ther,
David bought some **dough**nuts for his **Dad**,
Muriel made some **mues**li for her **mo**ther
But **Ma**ry had no **mo**ney and she **just felt sad**.

Four-part alliteration

Now we drop the word *bought* and put in its place another alliterative word. This will give it a ONE two three ONE two three beat. Careful with the verbs se**lect**, co**llect** and de**li**ver, with stress on the second syllable and schwa in the first.

> **Vocabulary notes**
> *purchase*, *select* and *seek* (past = *sought*) are relatively formal verbs; their less formal equivalents are *buy*, *choose* (or *pick*) and *look for*; to *shift* = 'move from one place to another'; and a *dozen* = 12.

31

2/3

Kenneth	collected a	kilo of	cabbage.
Polly	purchased a	packet of	peaches.
Sally	sought a	sackful of	salad.
Dennis	delivered a	dozen	doughnuts.
Charles	chewed a	chunk of	chocolate.
Shirley	shifted a	shopful of	sugar.
Freddy	fried a	fridgeful of	fritters.
Tina	tasted a	tin of	tomatoes.
Salome	selected a	slice of	salami.
Patricia	picked a	pound of	potatoes.

Artful Arthur

This is the final part of 'The do-it-yourself tongue-twister' sequence. Of course each noun, adjective and verb is stressed. But in order to do this as a rhythmic chant there has to be four main beats (indicated in bold in the first few lines). And remember to link the words where necessary. You should be doing it automatically by now. So say:

Artful **Ar**thur **ar**gued for an **arm**ful of **ar**tichokes.

= /ˈɑːtfə ˈlɑːθə ˈrɑːgjuːd fərə ˈnɑːmfələ ˈvɑːtɪtʃəʊks/

Because the vocabulary is fairly difficult you will have to use a dictionary quite a lot in order to understand it. So we end up with two matching tasks to help you remember the meanings of most of the verbs and adjectives.

> **Vocabulary notes**
> These notes are just for the nouns; *cardamom, fenugreek* and *vanilla* are all used for flavouring food; *gazpacho* is a Spanish summer soup, made with tomatoes and cucumber; *nougat* is a type of sweet, or candy, from France; *clams* are shellfish; a *sliver* is a very thin slice; *sturgeon* and *tuna* are fish; *treacle* comes from sugar.

Artful **Art**hur **arg**ued for an **arm**ful of **art**ichokes.
Able **A**mos **ached** for an **a**cre of **a**pricots.
Barmy **Bar**bara **bar**gained for a **bas**ket of **ba**nanas.
Beautiful **Be**linda **boil**ed a **bar**relful of **beans**.
Brash Brenda **bran**dished a **brief**case full of **bran**.

Careful **Cath**erine **cooked** a **ki**lo of **cabb**ages.
Carmen calmly **cart**ed off a **cart**load of **car**damom.
Cheerful **Char**lie **chose** a **chew**y chunk of **choc**olate.
Clever **Chlo**e **clung** to a **clus**ter of **clams**.
Dirty **Dun**can **dreamed** of a **do**zen dainty **duck**-eggs.

Fragrant **Fre**da **fried** a **fridge** full of **frit**ters.
Furtive **Fred**dy **fon**dled a **fist**ful of **fen**ugreek.
Gorgeous **Ger**trude **gasped** for a **gal**lon of **gaz**pacho.
Greedy **Gren**ville **grasped** for a **gross** of **green grape**fruit.
Happy **Har**ry **hauled** away a **ham**per full of **ham**.

Jerky **Ger**ald **jug**gled with some **jars** of **jam**.
Lazy **Law**rence **lugged** away a **lor**ry-load of **let**tuce.
Little **Lo**la **lapped** up a **li**tre of **le**mon juice.
Merry **Mi**chael **munched** a **mil**ligram of **mince**.
Naughty **Nor**ma **gnawed** a knob of **nut**ty **nou**gat.

Posh Pa**tri**cia **pur**chased a **pound** of **Po**lish **peach**es.
Queasy **Quen**tin **quaffed** a **quar**ter-pint of **quince**-juice.
Sad Sally **sa**voured a **sack** full of **sand**wiches.
Sheepish **Shir**ley **shat**tered a **shop** full of **shell**-fish.
Sly Sa**lo**me **sliced** off a **sli**ver of sa**la**mi.

Spotty **Spen**cer **spat**tered a **spoon**ful of **spin**ach.
Stocky **Ste**phen **stood** on a **stone** of **stick**y **stur**geon.
Tiny **Ti**na **tast**ed a **tea**spoonful of **tu**na.

Tricky **Trev**or **trad**ed a **trunk**ful of **trea**cle.
Vicious **Vic**tor **van**ished in a **van** full of va**nil**la.
Weary **Wan**da **wad**ed in a **wag**gon load of **wa**tercress.

Task 12   Match the adjectives with their definitions or synonyms.

1 artful	a)	having a bad skin condition
2 able	b)	nice-smelling, perfumed
3 barmy	c)	really small
4 brash	d)	happy (possibly because of the effect of alcohol)
5 cheerful	e)	clever, full of tricks, cunning, sly
6 fragrant	f)	uncontrolled in one's movements, clumsy
7 furtive	g)	misbehaved, or possibly slightly improper
8 gorgeous	h)	happy, in a good mood
9 greedy	i)	capable, skilful, clever
10 jerky	j)	always wanting more things, especially to eat
11 merry	k)	really beautiful
12 naughty	l)	over-confident, loud, too full of oneself
13 posh	m)	mad, crazy, not all there
14 queasy	n)	dishonestly tricky, unwilling to confide in others
15 sad	o)	quite short, but well-built
16 sly	p)	feeling slightly sick, uneasy about a possible action
17 spotty	q)	deceitful, clever in cheating, difficult to handle.
18 stocky	r)	sly, not wanting to be seen, up to no good
19 tiny	s)	upper-class, over-conscious of one's importance
20 tricky	t)	unhappy, down in the dumps, miserable

Task 13   Match the verbs with their definitions or synonyms.

1	ache	a)	to transport
2	argue	b)	to breath in suddenly and loudly
3	bargain	c)	to cut a thin section from a loaf of bread, a cake, etc.
4	boil	d)	to grab and hold on to with one or both hands
5	brandish	e)	to wave in the air
6	cling	f)	to cook in water at 100 degrees Celsius
7	fry	g)	to hurt, be in pain, long for
8	fondle	h)	to bite steadily at something till it is worn away
9	gasp	i)	to drink steadily (old-fashioned)
10	grasp	j)	to try to get something for a lower price
11	haul	k)	to drink the way a cat does
12	juggle	l)	to eat or taste while enjoying the flavour
13	lug	m)	to hold tightly to something with both arms
14	lap	n)	to throw liquid or semi-liquid matter on to something
15	munch	o)	to move or transport with difficulty
16	gnaw	p)	to dispute, quarrel, disagree verbally
17	purchase	q)	to keep three or more objects in the air simultaneously
18	quaff	r)	to walk in liquid which comes up higher than the ankles
19	savour	s)	to stroke gently and affectionately
20	shatter	t)	to chew carefully and steadily, while making some noise
21	slice	u)	to disappear
22	spatter	v)	to break something fragile into many small pieces
23	vanish	w)	to cook in oil or fat
24	wade	x)	to buy

PART II Stress in words and phrases

In Part I, the following points were made about stress:

- In words of two or more syllables, one syllable is more important than the other(s). If all the other syllables are weak, then we can call this the **stressed syllable**.

- In words of three or more syllables we may have to distinguish three degrees of stress, however. The most important syllable will carry **primary stress**, the next in importance will carry **secondary stress** and the rest can be called **weak**.

- The weakest possible syllables contain the schwa vowel, the shortest and most common vowel sound in English.

- Grammatical items are usually weak, many of them containing schwa (though some may also have a strong form).

- Certain word-stress patterns are more common than others. Two-syllable verbs, for example, usually have the pattern ○■. Two-syllable nouns, by contrast, usually have the opposite pattern ■○.

In Part II, we will look in more detail at the rules for stress, both in words and in phrases. And we will see exactly when certain rules can be broken.

Chapter 2
Stress in verbs

Introduction

In this section, we will consider seven different stress patterns for verbs. Before we look at what the rules are, carry out the following introductory task.

Task 14 Read and listen to the verbs in the list below.

- Look at the tables, where you will find an example of the seven stress patterns.

- Place each verb in its correct place. (Two have already been put in as examples.)

Some patterns are easier to see (and hear) than others. The purpose of this task is for you to discover if there is any which cause you problems. Those are the ones that you will need to concentrate on.

clarify	pre-set	prefer	accelerate	contradict
wander	soften	enliven	refuse	sentimentalize
interfere	defuse	apologize	damage	collect
abolish	co-chair	identify	occupy	measure
undertake	circularize	defend	prepaint	consider
substitute	surrender	overwhelm	monopolize	determine
remove	demist	understand	worry	idolize

1 surprise	2 develop	3 reload	4 introduce
collect			contradict

5 tremble	6 estimate	7 realise

(Note that the numbers 1–7 correspond to the different subsections in this main section.)

Two-syllable verbs ○■

Most two-syllable verbs, as we have seen, start with a weakly stressed syllable. Here are the most common of these initial syllables, together with a selection of the verbs containing them. They are grouped by vowel.

those containing schwa

a~ ab~ co~ com~ con~ for~ o~ ob~ per~ po~ pro~ su~ sur~ sus~

> abSORB / acCOUNT / acCUSE / alLOW / aMUSE / anNOUNCE/ aVERT / aVOID / colLECT / colLIDE / comMAND / comPARE / comPOSE / conDUCT / forGET / forGIVE / obJECT / obSERVE / ofFEND / perSUADE / poLICE / polLUTE / proDUCE / proTECT / subSIDE / subJECT / sugGEST / surPRISE / susPECT

those containing short /ɪ/

en~ ig~ im~ in~

> enDURE / enGAGE / igNORE / imPLY / imPORT / inCREASE / inFECT / inCLUDE / inVITE

those containing short /ɪ/, though schwa is an alternative

be~ de~ dis~ e~ pre~ re~ se~

> beCOME / beHAVE / beLIEVE / deBATE / deCIDE / deFY / deNY / deRIVE / deVOTE / disTRACT / enDURE / enQUIRE / eQUIP / esCAPE / preFER / prePARE / preSENT / reCORD / reCITE / reGRET / reMOVE / reFER / reSTORE / seCURE / seDATE

> **Note:** this group includes a fairly large category of verbs (conVICT / conTRAST / deCREASE / ferMENT / reCORD / imPORT / inCREASE / reBEL / perVERT / obJECT / subJECT) where the corresponding nouns have the opposite stress pattern: ■○. See Chapter 3.

Three-syllable verbs ○■○

There are fewer ○■○ than ○■ verbs. Most start with one of the weak initial syllables you have just met:

> aBOlish / acCOMplish /asSEMble / aWAKen / beWILder / conSIder / conTINue / deTERmine / deVElop / enCOUrage / reSEMble / surRENder

> **Note:** that most of these verbs end with a syllable that is normally weak: *~er, ~en, ~ish, ~age, ~it*. There will be more about final syllables on page 28.

Task 15   Listen to the following recording.

There is a series of sentences, each containing one of the verbs you have just met. There is no rhyme this time, but each sentence has the same beat, with a strong syllable followed by two weak ones.

ONE	2	3	ONE	2	3	ONE	2	3	ONE	2	(and)
DAH	du	du	DAH	du	du	DAH	du	du	DAH	du	(and)
Con	rad	com	posed	a	con	cert	o	for	trum	pet	
Ann	ie	a	nounced	she	had	wri	tten	a	nov	el	

Rhymes and Rhythm

You can only keep to the beat if you remember that each of the verbs starts with a really weak syllable. But it's time to mention one more thing about the stressed syllables: they are not just louder and longer than the weak ones; they are usually different in **pitch**. That is to say, that they are often higher or lower than the surrounding unstressed syllables. Not only that: a stressed syllable can change pitch, can go down or up smoothly.

Before you repeat the various poems, chants, raps and so on in this book, you should do two things: listen to the **rhythm** of course, make sure you hit the stresses and shorten the weak syllables; but you also have to listen to the **music** of the language, to the intonation (i.e. the way the voice goes up and down). So the sentence we have just looked at can be thought of as:

Conrad composed a concerto for trumpet

if we only think of the rhythm. But we must not forget that it may also sound like:

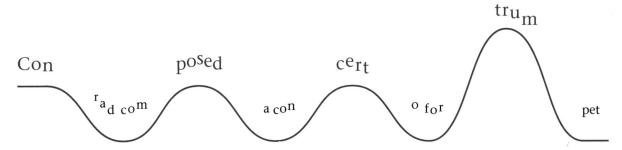

Now you have a choice. You can just listen to the sentences and repeat them. But, if you want to do some vocabulary practice first, try to match the beginnings (1–16) and endings (a–p) of the sentences in the word box below, **then** listen to the recording.

And when you repeat the sentences, do not be fooled by the spelling of names and verbs at the start of each sentence. Pairs such as *Percy/persuade* and *Connie/conduct* may look as if they contain the same vowel sound. Listen carefully, however. Each name starts with a stressed syllable, so the vowel sound in the name is always stronger than the weak vowel sound in the first syllable of the verb! Thus *Connie* = 'kɒni, whereas *conduct* = kən'dʌkt.

1 Percy persuaded	a) a vaccine for polio
2 Colin collected	b) a symphony orchestra
3 Dennis developed	c) she had written a novel
4 Reggie restored	d) to start up a business
5 Betty became	e) all the frescos in Florence
6 Oscar objected	f) a major catasrophe
7 Benny behaved	g) the troops to surrender
8 Avril averted	h) a classical record
9 Annie announced	i) all the men who'd betrayed him
10 Esther escaped	j) a quite famous celebrity
11 Desmond devoted	k) when others accepted
12 Rita recorded	l) a peaceful solution
13 Forster forgave	m) in a confident manner
14 Connie conducted	n) from a prisoner of war camp
15 Debbie decided	o) his life to the people
16 Susie suggested	p) some marvellous furniture

•■(○) verbs with a true prefix as first syllable

In most ○■ and ○■○ verbs, the weak initial syllable comes from a preposition in Latin. In English, the original meaning is often hidden. The fact that *sub~*, for example, originally meant 'under' is not clear in such words as *submit* or *subject* (though it is clearer in words such as *subsection* or *submarine*).

In some verbs, by contrast, the original meaning is still very clear. In such cases, we can describe the first syllable as a true **prefix**. (The weaker equivalents may be thought of as **semi-prefixes**.) True prefixes have strong vowels and will be transcribed showing **secondary** stress within the word. For example:

prefix	meaning	pron.	examples	
re~	'again'	/riː/	reload = /ˌriːˈləʊd/	rehouse = /ˌriːˈhaʊz/
de~	'removing'	/diː/	debug = /ˌdiːˈbʌg/	defuse = /ˌdiːˈfjuːz/
co~	'with'	/kəʊ/	cohabit = /ˌkəʊˈhæbɪt/	co-chair = /ˌkəʊˈtʃeə/
pre~	'before'	/priː/	preload = /ˌpriːˈləʊd/	preset = /ˌpriːˈset/

Be careful, however. Each of the above four has a weaker version, where the original meaning is less clear. Look at the following examples.

with prefix		with 'semi-prefix'	
repaint	= /ˌriːˈpeɪnt/	remove	= /rɪˈmuːv/ or /rəˈmuːv/
reset	= /ˌriːˈset/	reject	= /rɪˈdʒekt/ or /rəˈdʒekt/
reform	= /ˌriːˈfɔːm/	reform	= /ˌriˈfɔːm/ or /ˌrəˈfɔːm/
	(= form again)		(= improve, rectify)
demist	= /ˌdiːˈmɪst/	deceive	= /dɪˈsiːv/ or /dəˈsiːv/
deselect	= /ˌdiːˈsəˈlekt/	defend	= /dɪˈfend/ or /dəˈfend/
co-exist	= /ˌkəʊɪgˈzɪst/	collide	= /kəˈlaɪd/
co-chair	= /ˌkəʊˈtʃeə/	command	= /kəˈmɑːnd/
pre-pay	= /ˌpriːˈpeɪ/	prepare	= /prɪˈpeə/ or /prəˈpeə/
pre-paint	= /ˌpriːˈpeɪnt/	prefer	= /prɪˈfɜː/ or /prəˈfɜː/

> **Note** that the negative prefixes, such as *un~*, *mis~* and *dis~*, may also carry secondary stress within the word. E.g., unˈburden/ unˈsettle / disˈcourage / disˈfigure / disˈcredit / misˈmanage, and so on.

Three-syllable verbs •○■

In these verbs, the primary stress is on the third syllable and the middle syllable is very weak (usually containing schwa). But there is a noticeable secondary stress on the first syllable. This happens for one of three reasons:

a) The verb starts with a two-syllable prefix, for example:

ˌintroˈduce / ˌcontraˈdict / ˌoverˈwhelm / ˌunderˈstand

b) A prefix is added to a regular ○■ verb, for example:

ˌdisaˈppoint / ˌreabˈsorb / ˌdisaˈllow / ˌrecoˈmmend

c) There are two monosyllabic prefixes, for example:

ˌcoinˈcide / ˌappreˈhend / ˌcompreˈhend

■○ verbs

> If a verb has this pattern it is due to the presence of a final syllable which is always weak, causing the previous syllable to be stressed.

This rule applies whatever the number of syllables and overrides the general rule that two-syllable verbs tend to have the ○■ pattern. In the following tables, you will find the most common of these weak final syllables, together with their pronunciation and a selection of words containing them.

~le -el -al /əl/ or /l/	~on ~en /ən/ or /n/	~er ~our ~or /ə/	~sure ~ture /ʃə/ /ʒə/ /tʃə/
people	reckon	cater	censure /ʃə/
settle	beckon	wander	treasure /ʒə/
tremble	soften	favour	pleasure /ʒə/
quarrel	weaken	savour	measure /ʒə/
pedal	threaten	answer	picture /tʃə/
rival	listen	spatter	capture /tʃə/

~ow /əʊ/	~age /ɪdʒ/	~ish /ɪʃ/	~it /ɪt/	~y /i/
follow	damage	vanish	edit	envy
hollow	manage	banish	posit	tidy
borrow	ravage	finish	debit	worry
pillow	savage	nourish	credit	scurry
mellow	pillage	flourish	limit	query
		relish	profit	chivvy

> A number of comments have to be made about verbs with these endings, however.
>
> - In many cases (*people, pedal, credit, query, savage, finish, hollow, favour, treasure*, etc.) these verbs can also function as nouns. This particular stress rule applies whatever the class of word.
>
> - You have to be careful about word endings. The letters *~er* may well end a word without being a suffix. In ○■ verbs such as deter, inter, refer, confer and defer, for example, it is the elements *ter* and *fer* that are units, not *~er*.
>
> - Be careful with *~jure*, too. In words such as abjure: injure, perjure, conjure (= 'do tricks' – pronounced /ˈkʌndʒə/), conjure (= 'ask solemnly' – pronounced /ˌkənˈdʒʊə/) the *jure* element forms the unit. Confusion with the regular *ure* ending seems to be the cause of the inconsistency in pronunciation.
>
> - And not all verbs ending in *~it* have a final weak syllable. A number, including permit, omit, transmit, remit and submit are standard ○■ verbs, since the *mit* element is the unit (c.f., *mission* in the noun derivants).
>
> - Most established words in *~age* have the short /ɪdʒ/ ending. This is also the pronunciation of *~age* as a suffix (in, for instance, *seepage, footage, shrinkage*, etc.). But more recent borrowings from French (arbitrage / triage / corsage / camouflage, etc.) tend to end in the much longer /ɑːʒ/). And *garage* varies between the two, being pronounced in a variety of ways, including: /ˈgærɑːdʒ/, /ˈgærɪdʒ/, /gəˈrɑːʒ/ and /gəˈrɑːdʒ/.
>
> - Finally, be careful with allow.

(○)■○○ verbs

Some suffixes cause the main stress to fall on the syllable two from the end (the 'ante-penultimate'). This happens however many syllables come before the stress.

~ate /eɪt/[1]	~ute /juːt/ or /tʃuːt/	~ify /ɪfaɪ/	~iply ~upy /ɪplaɪ/ /ʊpaɪ/
CONgregate	iNstitute	dIGnify	mulTIply
eStimate	CONstitute	clARify	Occupy
faScinate	subStitute	amPLify	
aSSIMilate	proStitute	fORtify	
aCCElerate		iDENtify	
neGOtiate		perSOnify	

Verbs derived from nouns or adjectives by means of the suffix /aɪz/

A large number of verbs are derived from nouns and adjectives by means of this suffix. The verbs keep the main stress of the original word. Examples include:

original word →	derived verb	original word →	derived verb
SYMpathy	SYMpathize	CIRcular	CIRcularize
CRItic	CRIticize	real	REAlize
CApital	CApitalize	Organ	ORganize
aPOLogy	aPOLogize	chAracter	chAracterize
instiTUtional	instiTUtionalize	moNOpoly	moNOpolize

---

1 The <-ate> ending is often much weaker in nouns and adjectives. Thus *estimate* as a noun, and *approximate* as an adjective both end /ət/.

Chapter 3
Stress in nouns and adjectives

Who's who?

Chapter 2 asked you to think about the different stress patterns in verbs. Now we will do the same for nouns.

Task 16 Your task is to:

- Listen to and read the poem: 'Who's who?'. (As you can see, it is full of nouns with a variety of different syllables and stress patterns. But if you keep to the 3/4 beat you will have no choice but to hit the main stressed syllables correctly.)

- Pay special attention to the nouns listed below.

- Place the nouns in the table – where possible – according to their stress patterns. But note carefully! For the task in the previous section you had to find five verbs for each pattern. This time, however, you do not know how many words will go in each column. And also there are some odd ones out, i.e., some nouns which do not belong with the others in the table!

poet	neurotic	tailor	zoologist	selector
teacher	airman	cosmonaut	realist	diver
royalist	hack	geographer	philanthropist	confessor
doctor	wrestler	translator	astronaut	loyalist
barrister	idealist	photographer	broker	physician
balloonist				

a) healer	b) chairman	c) democrat	d) musician

e) technologist	f) loyalist	g) psychotic

When you repeat this poem, do not assume that syllables that are spelt the same are always pronounced the same. In Task 15 in the previous section, if you recall, you met various pairs of words including:

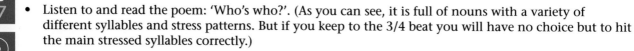

Percy / persuaded   Colin / collected

Dennis / developed   Avril / averted

In each case, the name contained a strong, stressed vowel, while the unstressed semi-prefix in the verb was considerably weaker.

There is a similar contrast in 'Who's who?', this time between the vowel sounds in pairs of nouns and names. For example:

Col's a collector
/'kɒlz ə kə'ləktə/

Con's a confessor
/'kɒnz ə kən'fesə/

Di's a director
/'daɪzə də'rektə/

Sol's a solicitor
/'sɒlz ə sə'lɪsɪtə/

The reason is quite clear; all the nouns are derived from verbs and retain the initial weak syllable. (For more details, see below.)

> **Vocabulary notes**
> *barrister* = a lawyer who can appear in a higher court; *boozer* = a person who likes alcoholic drinks (i.e., *booze*) far too much; *hack* = a derogatory term for a journalist; *proctor* = an official at the universities of Oxford and Cambridge; *solicitor* = a lawyer who advises clients, prepares legal documents, etc.

Who's who?

Tina's a **tea**cher, Priscilla's a **prea**cher,
Donald's a **doc**tor and Ted drives a **truck**.
Fred's a pho**to**grapher, Joe's a geo**gra**pher,
Barry's a **ba**rrister down on his **luck**.

Annie's an **a**narchist, Monty's a **mo**narchist,
Prue is a **proc**tor and Fred owns a **farm**.
Cy's a psy**cho**logist, Bill's a bi**o**logist,
Charley's a **char**mer who's run out of **charm**.

Col's a co**llec**tor and Di's a di**rec**tor,
Astrid's an **as**tronaut, Bas runs a **bank**.
Con's a con**fes**sor and Prue's a pro**fes**sor,
Cher owned a **ship** until (sadly) it **sank**.

Mag's a ma**gi**cian and Phil's a phy**si**cian,
Cosmo's a **cos**monaut circling the **moon**.
Ruby's a **rea**list, Ike's an i**dea**list,
Cindy's a **sing**er who can't hold a **tune**.

Ruth is a **wri**ter and Freddy's a **figh**ter,
Phil's a phi**lan**thropist handing out **cash**.
Sid's a psy**cho**tic and Norm's a neu**ro**tic,
Danny's a **dri**ver who's **scared** he might **crash**.

Walter's a **wai**ter and Tom's a trans**la**tor,
Aaron's an **air**man who **flies** through the **sky**.
Tammy's a **tai**lor and Willie's a **wha**ler,
Charlie's a **chair**man who **can't** tell a **lie**.

Benny's a **boo**zer and Lenny's a **lo**ser,
Sol's a so**li**citor, Chloe's a **clown**.
Eddie's an **edi**tor, Chrissie's a **cre**ditor,
Reg is a **wres**tler whose **job** gets him **down**.

Milly's a **mi**ller and Dave's a dis**ti**ller,
Kate's a co**me**dian, cracking a **joke**.
Dee is a **dea**ler and Harry's a **hea**ler,
Dave is a **di**ver who **can't** swim a **stroke**.

Ben's a ba**lloo**nist and Bet's a ba**ssoo**nist,
Freda's a **fe**minist, Harry's a **hack**.
Zac's a zo**o**logist, Tom's a tech**no**logist,
Brenda's a **bro**ker who's **just** got the **sack**.

Sal's a se**lec**tor and Den's a de**fec**tor,
Mike is a **mi**ner all **co**vered in **grime**.
Rita's a **roy**alist, Lita's a **loy**alist,
Paula's a **po**et whose **po**ems don't **rhyme**.

31

 nouns and adjectives

This stress pattern, which we may call front (or early) stress, is by far the most common for both nouns and for adjectives. Note how frequently nouns and adjectives of this type end with one of the weak syllables that we have already met in the case of ■○ verbs. E.g.,

lugg**age** / man**age** / spill**age** / foot**age** / mo**ther** / bo**ther** / fa**ther** / co**sy** / hu**rry** / frui**ty** / win**dow** / cal**low** / hol**low** / nim**ble** / han**dle** / par**tial** / pic**ture** / trea**sure** / sei**zure**.

Notable among nouns of this type are those 'agentive' nouns derived from monosyllabic verbs: div**er** / wait**er** / farm**er** / li**ar** / play**er** / teach**er** / act**or** / etc.

> **Note** this includes that set of nouns (im**port** / re**cord** / su**bject** / re**fund** / tran**sfer** / re**ject**, etc.) where the verbs with the same spelling have **late stress**, e.g., to im**port** / to re**cord** / to sub**ject** / to re**fund** / to transfer / to reject.

Nouns and adjectives derived from ○■ and ○■○ verbs

Most nouns and adjectives derived from ○■ and ○■○ verbs by the addition of suffixes keep the same main stress as the verbs. There may, however, be a change of vowel sound and, occasionally, of consonant, e.g., to suf**fice** / suf**fi**ciency; per**suade** / per**sua**sion. (If the stress does change, then this is usually due to the presence of a suffix that imposes its own stress pattern, as we shall see later in this section.)

> ac**com**plishment / ac**count**able / a**mus**ing / be**hav**iour / col**lec**tion / com**pa**rison / de**fec**tive / de**vel**opment / en**qui**ry / e**quip**ment / ex**cit**able / in**fec**tious / per**ver**sity / pre**sum**able / pro**duc**tion / re**hear**sal / re**sem**blance / suf**fi**ciency / trans**fer**ral

This type again includes a large number of agentive nouns such as:

> ac**count**ant / an**noun**cer / be**liev**er / en**qui**rer / of**fen**der / in**qui**rer / in**hab**itant / pro**duc**er / pro**tec**tor / sur**vey**or

Nouns and adjectives derived from ■○ verbs

Nouns and adjectives derived from ■○ verbs also tend to keep the stress pattern of the original verbs. For example:

> set**tle**ment / re**ck**oning / cen**sor**ship / man**age**ment / fel**low**ship

Agentive nouns include:

> cred**it**or / ed**it**or / fol**low**er / sof**ten**er / man**ag**er / trea**sur**er / wan**der**er

Stress-imposing suffixes

There are a number of suffixes which determine the stress pattern of nouns.

~ion, ~ian = /ən/ or /n/

In nouns ending with *ion*, or *ian* the main stress falls on the syllable before the end, no matter how many syllables. Where these suffixes are found in words of four or more syllables, then there is a clear secondary stress:

nation / fusion / option / Asian / confusion / adoption / musician / technician / ˌcondemˈnation / ˌdisiˈllusion / ˌcontraˈdiction / ˌcompreˈhension / ˌintroˈduction / ˌindeˈcision / ˌproseˈcution / ˌsubstiˈtution / ˌaggraˈvation / conˌgratuˈlation / ˌmultipliˈcation / ˌrecommenˈdation / ˌrealiˈsation / ˌqualifiˈcation / ˌsimplifiˈcation / ˌmagnifiˈcation

> **Note** how the syllable given secondary stress is usually that carrying main stress in the base verb, for example:
>
> | ~ate | conˈgratulate | conˌgratuˈlation |
> |------|---------------|------------------|
> | ~ify | ˈmagnify | ˌmagnifiˈcation |
> | ~ize | ˈrealize | ˌrealiˈzation |

~y (•)(○)(○)■○○

There are a large number of suffixes ending with *y*, corresponding to very weak /ɪ/. The preceding syllable also contains a very weak syllable, so the main stress comes two from the end, however long the word. These are similar in stress patterning to ~ly adverbs, a selection of which are included for comparison.

A very high proportion of these nouns are formal and/or scientific or technical, containing such suffixes as: ~ory, ~opy, ~ocy, ~acy, ~apy, ~ary, ~athy, ~omy, ~ogy, ~ophy, ~aphy, ~atry, and ~ity.

■○○

therapy / ivory / history / secretary / mystery / surgery / apathy / sympathy / lavatory / gracefully / feelingly / hurriedly / seemingly / mercifully

○■○○

identity / society / psychiatry / security / psychology / philanthropy / biography / modernity / obituary / laboratory / authority / amazingly / politically / believably

> **Note** this is the same stress pattern found in a number of four-syllable words ending in ~e, also corresponding to short /ɪ/. They include: aˈpostrophe, eˈpitome, caˈtastrophe and hyˈperbole.

●○■○○

ˌincaˈpacity / ˌcapaˈbility / ˌelecˈtricity / ˌcardiˈology / ˌphysiˈology / ˌunderˈstandably / ˌunbeˈlievably /

●○○■○○

ˌautobiˈography / ˌparapsyˈchology

> **Note** that some words ending in ~y (including *lavatory*, *literacy* and *secretary*) may have four syllables when spoken slowly. But in fast speech, what is called **compression** may take place. This means that the schwa syllable may be elided, reducing the word to three syllables, possibly to fit other words with this pattern. In fact, the middle schwa syllable in three syllable words, including *history* and *mystery* may similarly disappear.

For example:

Item		
lavatory	'lævətərı	'lævətrı
literacy	'lıtərəsı	'lıtrəsı
secretary	'sekrətəri	'sekrətrı
history	'hıstərı	'hıstrı
mystery	'mıstərı	'mıstrı

~ographer, ~onomer, ~onomist, ~iatrist

The very productive ~y group (see page 81) includes those learned suffixes: ~ology, ~onomy, ~ography and ~iatry. These have corresponding agentive nouns with the same stress pattern, such as:

> phot**O**grapher / bi**O**grapher / a**stro**nomer / bi**O**logist / psy**chia**trist / e**co**nomist / a**gro**nomist / ˌhagi'**O**grapher / ˌparapsy'**cho**logist / etc.

> **Note** that the syllable following the main stress always contains schwa; thus phot**O**grapher = /fə'tɒɡrəfə/; a**gro**nomist = /ə'ɡrɒnəmɪst/.

~ese /iːz/

The ~ese suffix is found in a number of nationality words (including Chi**nese** / Japa**nese** / Vietna**mese**) as well as a few other words such as journa**lese**.

~esque /esk/ and ~ette /et/

These suffixes are fairly rare. The first is used to derive adjectives from a number of proper names, to give the meaning 'similar to, in the style of', e.g., *Kafkaesque* / *Goyaesque* / *Chaplinesque*. (It is also found in a few other adjectives and nouns, such as *picturesque* and *humoresque*.) The second is found as a diminutive suffix in such words as *cigarette*, *kitchenette*, *lecturette* and *laundrette*.

> **Note** that ~ese, ~esque and ~ette impose a secondary stress two syllables before the main stress: e.g., ˌjapa'**nese** / ˌpictu'**resque** / ˌciga'**rette**.

~ic, ~ics, ~ical, ~icist

These related suffixes, all containing *ic*, affect the stress pattern of a large number of nouns and adjectives. The rule is that main stress falls on the syllable immediately before. For example:

> ■○(○)
> **pu**blic(ist) / **cy**nic(al) / **to**pic(al) / **lo**gic(al) / **o**ptic(al) / **phy**sic(al) / **phy**sicist / **tra**gic / **cri**tic(al) / **cla**ssic(al) / **eth**nic

○■○(○)

ceramic(s) / ceramicist / electric(al) / cosmetic(s) / dynamic / historic(al) / artistic / pathetic / political / illogical

Exceptions politic(s) / lunatic / Arabic

●○■○(○)

ˌmathe'matics / ˌperi'odic(al) / ˌeco'nomic(s) / ˌeco'nomic(al) / ˌmeta'physics / ˌmeta'physical / ˌanaes'thetic / ˌoce'anic / ˌaca'demic / ˌmathe'matical / ˌastro'nomical / ˌcate'goric(al)

●○○■○

ˌgeria'trician / ˌpaedia'trician

~ist

This is used to derive adjectives from:

- **nouns:** machinist / balloonist / bassoonist / etc.; or
- **adjectives:** realist / loyalist / royalist / idealist / etc.

Chapter 4
Stress in compounds and phrases

Introduction

Compounds are composed of more than one word or element, whether written as one word or not. And it is the main syllable in the first element of compounds that has primary stress.

Most compound nouns are made up of two elements, usually **noun + noun**. For example:

postman / policeman / teapot / classroom / 'bus,stop / schoolgirl / landlady / bookshop / 'evening ,dress / hitchhiker / mathe'matics ,teacher / 'tennis ,player / 'English ,teacher (= teacher of English) / 'visitors ,book / 'children's ,home / etc.

But other combinations of elements are possible.

adjective + noun (very common)

redhead / greenback / shortbread / longboat / greenhouse / hardware / shorthand / smalltalk / broadside / hotspot / the ,White ,House / six-pack / etc.

gerund + noun (very common)

dining room / swimming pool / baking powder / moving van / breathing space / running track / ironing board / skipping rope / winning post / etc.

verb + particle (increasingly common)

take off / shutdown / standby / sit-in / putdown / follow-up / walkout / flyover / drive-in / talkback / turn up / wind-up / flyby / breakthrough / sit up / stop over / hand over / etc.

verb + noun (not very common)

cut-throat / driveway / runway / swimwear / etc.

particle + verb (not very common)

offcut / input / offspring / overpass / underwear / bypass / etc.

Two elements from Latin or Greek (very common, especially in formal and/or scientific language)

acrobat / photograph / telephone / synonym / symphony / microphone / homophone / technocrat / gramophone / isobar / paragraph / thermostat / etc.

The meaning of most noun + noun compounds is usually quite clear; both constituents are ordinary English words and the compound is the sum of both words. Thus a *bookshop* is 'a shop where you buy books', a *bus stop* is 'a place where buses stop'.

The meaning of element + element compounds is usually less obvious. However, words such as *autograph, biopsy* and *telephone* contain highly meaningful elements: *auto* = 'self'; *graph* = 'writing'; *bio* = 'life'; *tele* = 'far' and *phone* = 'sound'.

The meanings of elements such as these are well worth knowing. They are only occasionally found as independent words. In combination, however, they produce several thousand three-syllable words, all with front stress and a very weak second syllable. (Of course, they are found in longer words, too; an *autobiography* – 'self' + 'life' + 'writing' – is 'an account of a person's life written by the person themselves'.) Since these elements are often neglected, I have written a poem to help you learn a number of them.

Task 17   Recreate the following poem.

Poems are often divided into separate stanzas (also called, verses). The following poem is written in what is known as rhyming couplets. (A couplet is a two-line stanza, so rhyming couplets are couplets where the rhyme scheme is AA, BB, CC, etc.) Here are the first two couplets of the poem:

An aCrobat is agile and can somersault and leap;
An OCtopus is something you might see beneath the deep.

A therMostat is useful to control the rate of heat;
A metronome is what you need to help you keep the beat.

As you can see, each line contains the definition of a three-syllable classical compound. (With front stress, of course.) Each compound is in its correct position in the poem below, but the definitions have been jumbled up. Your task is to:

• listen to the poem once or twice to get the rhythm;

• use a good dictionary to check the meaning of each compound;

• find the continuation which matches the meaning of the compound;

• re-create the poem.

Vocabulary notes

anthrop	= 'human'	anthropoid, philanthropist, etc.
aqua	= 'water'	aquatic, aquaduct, etc.
astr	= 'star'	astroid, astro-physics, astronaut, etc.
auto	= 'self'	automatic, automobile, etc.
chrom	=' colour'	monochromatic, polychromatic, etc.
cide	= 'kill'	homicide, regicide, germicide, etc.
duc	= 'lead, take'	duct, deduct, conduct, deduce, etc.
cosm	= 'world'	cosmic, microcosm, etc.
glot	= 'language'	glottis, polyglot, monoglot, etc.
gogue	= 'leader'	pedagogue, demagogue, etc.
graph	= 'writing'	telegraph, graphic, paragraph, etc.
homo	= 'same'	homophone, homograph, homosexual, etc.
hydro	= 'water'	hydroelectric, dehydrate, hydrogen, etc.
hypno	= 'sleep'	hypnosis, hypnotherapy, etc.
micro	= 'small'	microphone, microscopic, microcosm, etc.
mono	= 'one'	monocle, monotonous, monocellular, etc.
morph	= 'shape'	amorphous, morphology, anthropomorphic, etc.
naut	= 'sail, travel'	nautical, cosmonaut, astronaut, etc.
oid	= 'shaped like'	anthropoid, spheroid, ovoid, humanoid, etc.
ped	= 'child'	pedagogue, paediatrics, pederast, etc.
		(NB *ped* also = 'foot', as in pedal, pedestrian)
peri	= 'around'	perimeter, periscope, perigastric, etc.
phone	= 'sound'	telephone, phonetics, microphone, etc.
photo	= 'light'	photograph, photosensitive, etc.
poly	= 'many'	polymorph, polyglot, polytheism, etc.
reg	= 'king'	regicide, regal, reign, etc.
scope	= 'vision'	telescope, microscope, etc.
tele	= 'far'	telescope, telephone, telegram, etc.
via	= 'road'	viaduct, viable, deviate, etc.

37

An acrobat is agile

An acrobat is agile and can somersault and leap;
An octopus is something you might see beneath the deep.

A thermostat is useful to control the rate of heat;
A metronome is what you need to help you keep the beat

1 A periscope is	a) something that can take on many shapes
2 A chromosome is	b) pick up every single word you say
3 A homophone's	c) a type of boat that skims across the sea
4 A telegram is	d) useful if you want to see a wreck
5 A polymorph is	e) for people who like dancing every day
6 The anthropoids are	f) occasionally worn by certain men
7 A telephone's	g) teach your little children, for a fee
8 A microphone can	h) found in living cells, just like a gene
9 A hydrofoil's	i) what will bring you water from afar
10 A pedagogue will	j) visit Venus, Jupiter or Mars
11 A cosmonaut might	k) never even dream of such a thing
12 An astronaut could	1) something you can use to trap a liar
13 A germicide is	m) someone who has killed a queen or king
14 A discotheque's	n) known to certain people as a 'snap'
15 A photograph is	o) written with a pencil or a pen
16 A hypnotist is	p) useful if you're in a submarine
17 A polyglot might	q) something that you might send to your mother
18 A bathysphere is	r) go much farther, even to the stars
19 The dinosaurs	s) shaped like us: the monkeys and the apes
20 while hydrogen and oxygen	t) understand both Japanese and Czech
21 An aquaduct is	u) by contrast, is more useful for your car
22 A viaduct,	v) someone who could help you take a nap
23 An autograph is	w) things you shouldn't throw into a fire
24 A monocle's	x) combine as H_2O
25 A polygraph is	y) a word that sounds exactly like another
26 and aerosols are	z) for talking to a person far away
27 A regicide is	aa) what can help to keep disease at bay
28 A monarchist would	bb) all died out several million years ago

And if this kind of lexicon is hard to comprehend,
then you had better try to get a teacher as a friend.

Stress in noun phrases

Two-word noun phrases tend to have **late stress**. We can say that, within the phrase, the first element has secondary stress, while the second has primary stress.

Many two-word phrases consist of the same elements found in compounds: noun + noun; adjective + noun; gerund + noun. And sometimes, the actual words used are the same in both compound and phrase. So it is worth looking at the underlying differences in meaning.

Task 18   Look at the following pairs of sentences. In each pair, the first sentence contains a phrase, and the second a compound. See if you can work out the differences in meaning.

1   She was wearing a ˌcotton 'dress.
    They work in a 'cotton ˌfactory.

2   You should be wearing ˌrubber 'gloves.
    I've just bought a rubber ˌplant.

3   Would you like a ˌmeat 'pie?
    He works as a 'meat ˌpacker.

4   I've invited two friends, an ˌEnglish 'teacher (and a French scientist).
    She works as an 'English ˌteacher.

5   We saw a beautiful ˌblack 'bird.
    We saw a beautiful 'blackbird.

6   Can you see that ˌwhite 'house over there?
    The US President lives in the 'White ˌHouse.

7   It's dangerous to jump on to a ˌmoving 'train.
    We have so much furniture we'll need a 'moving ˌvan.

8   I put all my money on the ˌwinning 'horse!
    The horses are very close to the 'winning ˌpost.

So it seems that phrases tend to mean either:

1   X is made of Y   (a *meat pie, cotton dress, rubber gloves*, etc.) or

2   X is Y   (*an English teacher*, a *winning horse*, a *white house*, etc.)

And compounds, by contrast, tend to mean:

1   X is a special type of Y   (a *blackbird, the White House*, etc.)

2   X is for Y   (a *cotton factory, dining room, moving-van*, etc.)

3   an X of Y   (a *meat packer, an English teacher*)

Note these are tendencies that cover the great majority of cases. But be careful of the words *cake, juice* and *water*. They do not obey the X is made of Y rule. For example:

phrases: a ˌcheese 'sandwich / an ˌapple 'pie / a ˌbarley 'loaf

compounds: a 'cheeseˌcake / an 'orange ˌjuice / some 'barley ˌwater

Also the sequences ˌwinter 'dress / ˌsummer 'suit / ˌspring 'hat, etc., are phrases, although they could be explained as meaning 'a dress for the winter', 'a suit for the summer', etc.

Note also that late stress is found in such phrases as:

a ˌcup of 'tea / a ˌpint of 'milk / a ˌpound of 'butter / ˌrock and 'roll / ˌfish and 'chips / ˌboys and 'girls, etc.

Note, finally, that sequences may consist of a combination of phrase and compound. Thus the phrase ˌhot 'water can be the first part of the compound ˌhot 'water ˌbottle. By contrast, the compound 'elderflower can be the first part of the phrase ˌelderflower cham'pagne.

Task 19   **Here is a poem containing a number of noun compounds and phrases.**

- Read it first and see if you can identify which are the compounds and which are the phrases among the things which Alexandra buys.
- Then listen to it and see if your ears confirm what your eyes see.

Vocabulary notes

Clothes terms

The following three words are all from French: *brassiere* (worn to support the breasts); *lingerie* (= 'women's underwear'); a *negligee* (a light garment, usually worn over a night-dress). *Hose* is a technical term for socks, tights and stockings.

Acquire is a formal word meaning 'to get, obtain, receive'; *attire* is a very formal word meaning 'clothes'; *distraught* (rhymes with thought/taught/caught) = 'worried, nervous'; *expire* is a formal word meaning 'to die' (a visa or licence can expire.); *flashy* means 'too bright, in bad taste'; to *hoard* = 'to hide something away' (a *hoard* is what is hidden); *hues* = 'colours'; something *illicit* is what you do not want people to know about; to *let* a person *down* = 'to disappoint them'; a *shopping spree* is when you spend a lot of money buying things; *sombre* is the opposite of 'bright'; *spouse* is a formal word meaning 'husband or wife'; *stifled* means 'cut off', as if a hand is put over your mouth.

A cautionary tale

One morning Alexandra Brown
got on the bus and went to town.
Convinced she looked a total mess
she thought she'd buy a cheapish dress.
But she had recently acquired
a credit card, and thus inspired
set off upon a shopping spree
from nine o'clock till half past three.

She started in a modest way;
a cotton skirt, in darkish grey.
But what it needed, so she felt,
would be a simple leather belt.
But when the belt was fastened tight
she thought it called for something bright;
a brooch, a ring, some earrings too,
two silken blouses, pink and blue.

And then, her shoes, a sombre green
were hardly worthy to be seen;
she really needed one more pair
(she scarcely had a thing to wear).
But hesitating which to buy
she finally decided, 'I
will take the black, the blue, the brown,
(they're always nice around the town)
and then those white ones, and the peach
(just right for summer on the beach).

And since I'd like to take up sport,
well then perhaps I think I ought
to buy myself some tennis shoes
and I suppose I'd better choose
some riding breeches and a skirt
with just a simple linen shirt.'

And so she went from store to store,
just thinking 'maybe one thing more'.
From Selfridges to C&A
(well, after all, no need to pay)
Armani, Harrods, BHS
'Well that's the lot', she thought, 'unless
I bought myself an evening gown.
I really can't let Crispin down.
A handbag, too', then for a laugh
she chose a rather flashy scarf.

'And that is that,' at last she thought
now feeling just a touch distraught.
'I'd better get home for my tea.
I wonder what the bill will be.'

The following month the bill appeared;
it was far worse than she had feared.
Ten thousand pounds and twenty p.
'Oh dear, 'she murmured, 'Goodness me!'
'Now what will Crispin think? Oh my!
He'll want to know the reason why.'
(She'd hidden all her things away,
afraid of what her spouse would say.)

Then suddenly she had a thought;
surely the things that she had bought
could all be taken back and then
things would be normal once again!

She rushed up to the second floor
and placed her hand upon the door
of that large wardrobe where she'd stored
the whole of her illicit hoard.
She grabbed the handle, gave a twist
with all the power of her wrist.

The door flew wide, and suddenly
out came a flood of lingerie,
of coats and hats and tights and shoes,
and brassieres of different hues,
of summer blouses, winter hose,
an avalanche of varied clothes,
of cashmere sweaters, fine and rare,
of overcoats and underwear.
She tried to scream, she tried to shout,
she tried to wave her arms about,
but under piles of mixed attire
she started slowly to expire.
Her final little cry of 'hey!'
was stifled by a negligee.

So when you're going out to shop
and want to ask for credit, stop!
Just listen carefully to my tip
and think before you sign the slip.

Stress in adjectival compounds and phrases

Adjectives, like nouns, can be found both in early stressed compounds and in late stressed phrases.

Adjectival compounds

Noun + adjective

They are so 'house-ˌproud they spend all their time cleaning and polishing.

He's broken his leg again. He's really 'accident-ˌprone.

Noun + gerund

That fruit is very 'thirst-ˌquenching.

The Grand Canyon is really 'awe-inspiring.

Noun (or particle) + past participle

After months at sea she was completely 'sun-tanned.

Stand up for yourself. You've been 'down-trodden all your life.

Shy? I was absolutely 'tongue-tied.

Adjectival phrases

Adjective + past participle

They're so ˌabsent 'minded they even forget their children's names!

They are so ˌlow-'paid they never go away on holiday.

I like my eggs ˌhard-'boiled, five minutes at least.

Adjective + gerund

You can relax with them. They're really ˌeasy-'going.

He's ˌgood-'looking with excellent dress-sense.

Adjective + noun

Her novels are really ˌfirst-'class, but her plays are pretty ˌsecond-'rate.

The job is really ˌhigh-'risk.

Adjective + adjective

Careful! That iron is ˌred-'hot!

He was lying in the road ˌdead 'drunk.

Adjective/past participle + particle

I've had enough. I'm really ˌfed-'up; completely ˌbrowned-'off!

I'm not just ˌtired-'out; I'm ˌall-'in.

Adverb + adjective/past participle

She's ˌfantastically 'clever and really ˌwell-'known.

His questions are always ˌcarefully 'chosen.

Particle + past participle

I like my meat ˌunder 'done but that was really ˌover-'cooked.

Three-word phrases

Don't let this go any further. It's strictly ˌoff-the-'record.

Their clothes are always ˌup to 'date.

The acting is inconsistent; very ˌhit and 'miss.

Noun + adjective

Their clothes were ˌbrand-'new.

Eat up or your food will be ˌstone-'cold.

All our eggs are ˌfarm-'fresh.

Noun + past participle

All our beer is ˌhome-'brewed and our pullovers are ˌhand-'knitted.

The knives and forks are ˌsilver-'plated.

She won't change her mind. She's really ˌiron-'willed.

As you can see, the choice between compound and phrase is clear except where you have **noun + adjective/past participle**. In such cases, you just have to learn the stress pattern when learning the item, I'm afraid.

> **Note** that adverbial phrases tend to have late stress, for example:
>
> He tripped and fell ˌhead-over 'heels.   We talked ˌround the 'clock.
>
> We rowed ˌdown 'stream.   Let's meet ˌhalf-'way.

Chapter 5
Stress patterns in words and phrases

Here are various stress patterns. Listen to the recording, then listen and repeat. Note that most patterns can be represented either by a single word or by a longer sequence: a phrase (or even a sentence).

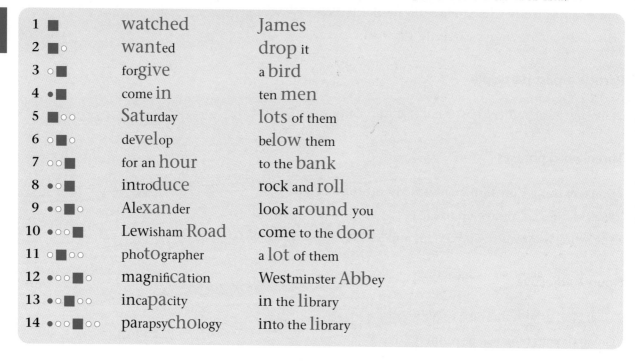

1 ■	watched	James	
2 ■○	wanted	drop it	
3 ○■	forgive	a bird	
4 ●■	come in	ten men	
5 ■○○	Saturday	lots of them	
6 ○■○	develop	below them	
7 ○○■	for an hour	to the bank	
8 ●○■	introduce	rock and roll	
9 ●○■○	Alexander	look around you	
10 ●○○■	Lewisham Road	come to the door	
11 ○■○○	photographer	a lot of them	
12 ●○○■○	magnification	Westminster Abbey	
13 ●○■○○	incapacity	in the library	
14 ●○○■○○	parapsychology	into the library	

Task 20   Now look at the following words, names and phrases below, read them aloud and number them according to their stress pattern based on the examples above.

somebody	police	photographic	Macbeth
go to the bank	stopped	Kensington High Street	follow
Vaughan	Hungary	defend	embargo
leather	Speaker's Corner	biology	tired out
Charing Cross	a big one	best results	maternity
institution	try a banana	Elizabeth	red hot
tomato	buy a new one	for a while	as a rule
Madonna	biographical	Leicester	hungry
conservative	Buckingham Palace	Royal Exchange	Peter Davidson
inner circle	offer him money	buy now	dead drunk
knives	all of the elephants	Michael	half a pound
Peru	geriatrician	after it	sympathy
through	half a sandwich	to the school	buy us some food
Iran	a pound of it	Madame Tussauds	give me a drink
a few	outer space	autobiography	sending a telegram
Manchester	next year	Trafalgar	the last of them
policeman	disability	come to the disco	Nelson's Column

Chapter 6
Stress shift

So far, we have assumed that each word could only be stressed in one way. But there are circumstances in which the rules of stress are broken and stress can shift from its normal place.

Contrastive stress shift

First, any stress pattern can change if we want to show a particular contrast. Thus the word *policeman* is normally pronounced /pə'liːsmən/, with main stress on the first element, as is usual in compounds. But see what happens in the following exchange.

> 1 So a po**lice**man came to see you, did he? (= /pə'liːsmən/)
>   No, not a police**man**; it was a police**wo**man. (= /pəˌliːs'mæn/)

The contrast between *man* and *woman* overrides the normal rule. Here are some more examples of contrastive stress shift.

> 2 So you've bought a new **tele**phone. (= /'teləfəʊn/)
>   No, not a tele**phone**, a tele**scope**. (= /ˌtelə'fəʊn/)
>
> 3 I gather that John's a **phy**sics teacher. (= /ə 'fɪzɪks ˌtiːtʃə/)
>   No, he's a physics **stud**ent, not a physics **teach**er. (= /ə ˌfɪzɪks 'tiːtʃə/)
>
> 4 You're a com**put**er operator, I understand.
>   No, not a computer **op**erator, a computer **pro**grammer.
>
> 5 Would you like a cheese **sand**wich?
>   I'd rather have a to**ma**to sandwich.
>
> 6 Would you like to sit out**side**?
>   Is it possible to sit **in**side, instead?
>
> 7 Did you buy that cotton **shirt** you were looking at?
>   No, I changed my mind and bought a **silk** shirt.
>
> 8 Do you fancy fish and **chips**?
>   I'd rather have **chick**en and chips, I think.
>
> 9 As a writer, I'd rate him first-**class**. What do you think?
>   Closer to **third**-class, in my opinion.

Let's see what has happened to the **stress patterns** in the above examples.

* Compounds can lose their front stress, which can give them the stress pattern associated with phrases.

  'telephone   tele'phone (2)

  'phySics ˌteacher   ˌphysics 'teacher (3)

* Or the opposite can happen, with phrases having the pattern associated with compounds.

  toˌmato'sandwich   to'mato ˌsandwich (5)

  ˌchicken and 'chips   'chicken and ˌchips (8)

But be careful. Spoken language is more than just stress, as has already been said. So we have to do more than just shift the stress.

Here are some of those sequences again. Listen once more, this time paying particular attention to the intonation in the second sentence of each example.

1 So a policeman came to see you, did he?

No, not a policeman; it was a policewoman.

2 So you've bought a new telephone.

No, not a telephone, a telescope.

3 I gather that John's a physics teacher.

No, he's a physics student, not a physics teacher.

4 You're a computer operator, I understand.

No, not a computer operator, a computer programmer.

The first speaker in each case not only uses the regular stress pattern for *policeman, telephone, physics teacher* and *computer operator*; s/he also uses a **falling tone**. This is the normal tone in such cases; **new** information is being introduced into the conversation. But when the sequences are repeated by the second speaker, we have to note not only the shift of stress, but also the use of a **fall-rise tone**. This is because the items are now part of **old, shared** information. When the second speaker supplies **new** information (*policewoman, telescope, student, programmer*) s/he uses, as we might expect, the **falling** tone again.

So, from now on, do not pay so much attention to stress that you neglect intonation. In particular, when you listen to (and imitate) the poems in Part IV, make sure you concentrate not only on getting a feel for the rhythm of English; the music of English is there, too.

Forward stress shift

The second circumstance in which the stress can change is in accordance with what is happening in the rest of the sentence. Listen to the following sequences.

You need a **first**-class ticket to travel first-**class**.
Princess Elizabeth's a royal prin**cess**.
I live in Picca**dilly**, near **Picca**dilly Circus.
My friend's Chi**nese**, she's a **Chi**nese cook.
Her **six**teenth birthday is on the six**teenth**.
You're always inter**fering**, you **inter**fering fool!
I work out**doors**, I've got an **out**door job.
He's really **sharp**-eyed; he's a sharp-**eyed** guy.
She works part-**time**, she's got a **part**-time position.
I've got a **rent**-free house, I live rent-**free**.
He's a **small**-time gambler, really small **time**.
It's nine o'**clock**, let's listen to the **nine** o'clock news.
We must be demo**cratic**, take a **demo**cratic vote!
I agree abso**lutely**, I'm **abso**lutely sure.
The book's un**abridged**, it's the **un**abridged version.

Have you worked out what happens?

Most phrases, as we have seen, have late stress, as do a large number of words when in their dictionary form or at the end of a sequence. But **the stress shifts forward** when the phrase or word acts as a modifier within another phrase.[1]

---

1   This usually happens within noun phrases, but it can happen within other types of phrase. As you can see from the example of *absolutely sure*.

If the explanation sounds complicated, just listen and compare the two types in the following box.

word or phrase	longer phrase containing the original
ˌfirst-ˈclass	a ˌfirst-class ˈticket
a ˌprinˈcess	ˌPrincess Eˈlizabeth
ˌPiccaˈdilly	ˌPiccadilly ˈcircus
ˌChiˈnese	a ˌChinese ˈcook
ˌsixˈteenth	her ˌsixteenth ˈbirthday
ˌinterˈfering	you ˌinterfering ˈfool
ˌoutˈdoors	an ˌoutdoor ˈjob
ˌsharˈp-eyed	a ˌsharp-eyed ˈguy
ˌpart-ˈtime	a ˌpart-time poˈsition.
ˌrent-ˈfree	a ˌrent-free ˈhouse
ˌsmall ˈtime	a ˌsmall-time ˈgambler
ˌnine oˈclock	the ˌnine o'clock ˈnews.
ˌdemoˈcratic	a ˌdemocratic ˈvote
ˌunaˈbridged	the ˌunabridged ˈversion.
ˌabsoˈlutely	ˌabsolutely ˈsure

> The modifier in the right-hand column is marked as having secondary stress. That is to show what it does within the phrase; the primary stress comes in the main word of the phrase.

Task 21   Listen to and then repeat the following four-beat poem/chant. Note down every example of a phrase in which stress shift has taken place.

Vocabulary notes
There are several words associated with show business in general or rock/jazz music in particular. A *gig* is a concert or other event when you get paid to play; a *fan* is a person who likes your music; a *lick* is a musical phrase; you play the bass-drum by foot, using a *pedal*; to *hit it big* is to become popular and successful; the *stand* (or bandstand) is a raised platform where the band plays; to *get a hand* is to be clapped or applauded by the audience.

A long-haired drummer in a rock 'n' roll band

■   ■   ■   ■

1 I worked last night, played a one-night stand.
   I'm a long-haired drummer in a rock 'n' roll band.

2 It was a four-hour show, a first-rate gig.
   Some day soon we should be hitting it big.

3 The crowd all cheered, we got a well-earned hand;
   especially the drummer in the rock 'n' roll band.

4 A red-headed woman wearing high-heeled shoes
   helped a bald-headed fellow dance away his blues.

5 An unnamed fan clambered on the stand
   to try to reach the drummer of the rock 'n' roll band.

6 We were stone-cold sober, didn't touch a drop,
   had no time for drinking, we were playing non-stop.

7   It was positively great, it was absolutely grand
    to be drumming as a member of a rock 'n' roll band.

8   We played instrumental numbers, all the rock 'n' roll licks
    I smashed my bass-drum pedal and a dozen pairs of sticks.

9   They wouldn't let us go, we played longer than we planned.
    You'd think they'd never danced to a rock 'n' roll band.

10 Five, four, three, two a one-night stand.
    I'm a long-haired drummer in a rock 'n' roll band.

In this final section of Part II we have been looking at the ways in which the rules of stress can change.

But other things can change, too, especially in fast, informal speech. And that is what we will be looking at in Part III.

PART III Fast, natural speech

In Parts I and II we looked at the following areas: the importance of stress; vowel length; the way words link together; rules of stress, both in words and phrases; and the times when rules can be overridden.

All of the above are important, however slow or fast the rate of speaking, however formal or informal the occasion. What we have been looking at, in fact, are the things that you should do when speaking English if you want to be easily understood.

In Part III, we will look at what happens when English is spoken at normal, fast speed. Not in very formal contexts, such as making speeches or giving lectures, but in the normal, everyday situations of life.

Of course, you do not have to try to speak this fast. You can carry on speaking relatively slowly and – provided that you stress words and phrases accurately – people will understand your pronunciation.

But if you want to understand normal, fast English, then it is important for you to pay attention to what is covered here. And, of course, if you want to approach native-speaker speed, then you must practise what is covered here.

In other words: Parts I and II contain what will help you to be understood by us more easily. And this part contains what you must learn:

- if **you** want to understand **us**; and

- if you want to begin to really **sound** like us.

Chapter 7
Introduction to fast, natural speech

In a moment we will begin to look in detail at the different things that happen when we speak English fast. There is one thing that they all have in common: they make it **easier** to speak fast.

When we speak, we use a large number of different muscles, sometimes at the same time. And as we do with any type of repeated physical activity, we try to cut down on unnecessary movements; we take short cuts. The opening two tasks in this section are to see if you can hear some of the main differences between slow and fast speech. One of the things that happens, when we start to speak faster, is that certain sounds disappear.

Task 22 **You will hear the same passage read twice. First slowly, then fast. Listen to both versions carefully, then decide which sounds are heard in the slow version but not in the fast version.**

> The first girl and the first boy
>
> The second girl and the second boy
>
> The third girl and the third boy
>
> The next girl and the next boy
>
> The last girl and the last boy

Task 23 **The second thing that happens when we begin to speak fast is that certain sounds change. Listen again to the passage being read at both speeds and decide which sounds are different in the fast version.**

Tasks 22 and 23 showed the two main types of change that take place when we speak fast. And from now on, we will call these changes by their usual names. (Don't be worried about technical terms; there aren't many of them, they save a lot of time, and you will get used to them very quickly.)

Type 1 Elision
Elision is when a sound simply disappears (= **is elided**).

There is a small set of sounds – always the same – which tend to be elided when we speak fast, but only in a specific set of circumstances.

Type 2 Assimilation
Assimilation is what happens when a sound changes (= **is assimilated**) because of another sound. There are two main forms of assimilation:

- a sound changes to become more like the next sound; this is called **anticipatory assimilation**;

- two sounds join together to become a third sound; this is called **coalescent assimilation** (= the two sounds merge, or **coalesce**, to become one).

In the rest of Part III we will be looking in detail at elision and assimilation, but first, here is a version of the 'First girl, first boy' sequence, extended into a chant. Listen to it several times, then chant along with it. You will find that you can only keep up (i.e., chant at the same speed) if you do what a native speaker does: hit the stress correctly, weaken vowels where necessary, link, elide and assimilate. In particular, look out for the weak forms of *that*, *a*, *of* and *was*, all containing schwa.

Don't worry if you don't get the point of the elision and assimilation immediately; we will look at both of them later in this section.

Vocabulary notes

Cooking or preparing food
You *fry* food (eggs, meat, bread, etc.) in a *frying-pan* with fat or oil.
You *grill* food over or under direct heat. A barbecue is a type of *grill*.
You *slice* bread (cake, meat, etc.) with a knife. You can buy *sliced* bread and can eat a *slice of cake*. You *toast* slices of bread under a grill or in an electric *toaster* until they are brown. (Toasted bread is called *toast*.)

Talking
To *boast* is to talk with pride about what you do or own, about your family, etc.
To *mutter* is to talk quietly and indistinctly, so that people find it hard to understand.
To *trill* is to produce two different sounds very fast, rather like a bird.

The first girl said that she'd like a slice of bread.
The second girl muttered that she'd really like it buttered.
The third girl replied that she'd rather have it fried.
The next girl trilled that she much preferred it grilled.
The last girl was quiet ... but she was on a diet.

The first boy said that he'd like a slice of bread.
The second boy muttered that he'd really like it buttered,
The third boy replied that he'd rather have it fried.
The next boy trilled that he much preferred it grilled.
The last boy was quiet ... but he was on a diet.

Chapter 8
Elision

Elision of /t/ + /d/

In Task 22, we saw that in fast speech the sounds /t/ and /d/ were elided in contexts such as: *firs(t) girl / firs(t) boy / secon(d) girl / secon(d) boy.*

The context that is common to all four – and which makes elision likely – is that /t/ and /d/ were found:

a) at the end of a word; and

b) between two other consonants.

Task 24 Read the following sequences. See if you can identify where /t/ and /d/ elision can take place when they are read fast.

1 The morning was perfect.

2 It was a perfect morning.

3 It was a perfectly marvellous morning.

4 What does she want?

5 She wants ten pounds of butter.

6 I find it interesting, but he finds it boring.

7 We need to have the facts as soon as possible.

8 I don't usually watch television, but I watched four different programmes last night.

9 Jane hates fast food, so she won't want any burgers.

10 We're having roast beef with baked potatoes and beans.

Some effects of /t/ and /d/ elision

a) You hear the final /t/ and /d/ in the root of some words, but not when a suffix is added. For example:

without elision	with elision
It was perfect	It was perfec(t)ly marvellous
That's exact	That's exac(t)ly right
She's full of tact	She's very tac(t)ful
What does she want?	She wan(t)s some butter
One pound of butter	Ten poun(d)s of butter

b) Elision can also affect the ~ed for simple past and past participle. This means that, at speed, there may be no difference between present and past simple. (The context is what makes the difference clear, of course.)

slow version	fast version
I watch television every day.	I watch television every day.
I watched television last night.	I watch(ed) television last night.
They crash the car regularly.	They crash the car regularly.
They crashed the car yesterday.	They crash(ed) the car yesterday.
I wash my hands before I have lunch.	I wash my hands before I have lunch.
I washed my hands before I had lunch.	I wash(ed) my hands before I had lunch.
They usually finish their work at six.	They usually finish their work at six.
They finished work early yesterday.	They finish(ed) work early yesterday.

c) Even the negative ~t may disappear at speed. For example:

slow version	fast version
I can't say	I can('t) say
I don't know	I don('t) know
Can't pay, won't pay.	Can('t) pay, won('t) pay.
They haven't finished work.	They haven('t) finish(ed) work.

d) Because of /t/ or /d/ elision a number of different words, when spoken at speed, can sound exactly the same. For example:

slow version	fast version
We need the facts today	We need the fac(t)s today = We need the fax today
I just saw the prints	I jus(t) saw the prin(t)s = I just saw the prince
Have you heard about the finds?	Have you heard about the fin(d)s = Have you heard about the fines?
Please buy some mints	Please buy some min(t)s = Please buy some mince
Cold storage	Col(d) storage = Coal storage
fast food	fas(t) food = farce food

Note that /t/ has a tendency to disappear even when it is not between two consonants. *Let's* go can be /les gəʊ/, sounding like *less go*, for example.

Task 25   Here are various compounds and phrases. In most of them elision of /t/ or /d/ is possible. See how quickly you can identify the ones where it is not possible.

software	compact disc	hardware
landmine	postman	loudspeaker
soundcheck	standby	childbirth
handcuffs	smart card	wildfire
word processor	old boy	best man
sandbag	eastbound	turned off

Elision of identical or similar consonants

Identical consonants

Concentrate on the final consonants in the following words:

lamp = /læmp/   six = /sɪks/

prime = /praɪm/   lettuce = /letəs/

Now see what tends to happen when these words are followed by another word starting with the same consonant.

very slow version	normal version
a lamp post = /ə ˈlæmp ˌpəʊst/	(sounds like) a lamb post = /ə ˈlæm ˌpəʊst/
six students = /ˌsɪks ˈstjuːdənts/	(sounds like) sick students = /ˌsɪk ˈstjuːdns/
Prime Minister = /ˌpraɪm ˈmɪnɪstə/	(sounds like) pry minister = /ˌpraɪ ˈmɪnɪstə/
lettuce salad = /ˌletəs ˈsæləd/	(sounds like) letter salad = /ˌletə ˈsæləd/

When two identical consonants meet, as in the above examples, then you are unlikely to produce both of them. And this is not limited to fast speech; even BSC newsreaders refer to the Prime Minister as the *pry minister*, (Check what *pry* means and you'll see why that amuses me.)

Again, it is a question of saving yourself effort. Take *lamp post;* in order to produce /p/ you have to: close your lips; gather air behind the place of closure; open the glottis (or it will sound like /b/); then release the lips. And to say /ˈlæmp ˌpəʊst/ you have to do this twice in rapid sequence. So what happens in the case of plosives, such as /p/, is that you do it just the once

With continuants (as in *Prime Minister*), the sound is lengthened slightly. Imagine it as *Prymmminister*.

Similar consonants

The above examples concerned the coming together of **identical** consonants. Elision also happens with what we can think of as similar consonants. This is not a technical term, but I use it to refer to sounds which are produced at or about the same point in the mouth: such as those found at the start of the following words: *dog* = /dɒg/; *table* = /teɪbl/; *chicken* = /tʃɪkɪn/; and *jar* = /dʒɑː/.

All of them are produced with the tongue making contact at more or less the same point: at or just behind the teeth-ridge. So it saves time, when these sounds meet, if the release of air is only made after the second has been produced. Thus *fried chicken*, instead of being pronounced /ˌfraɪd ˈtʃɪkɪn/, tends to sound like *fry chicken*, since the /d/ becomes part of the /tʃ/ of *chicken*.

Listen to the following, involving both identical and similar consonants.

very slow version	fast version	very slow version	fast version
a dark curl	a dar(k) curl	hard judges	har(d) judges
a dark girl	a dar(k) girl	soap powder	soa(p) powder
a good dog	a goo(d) dog	soap bowl	soa(p) bowl
a good time	a goo(d) time	this singer	thi(s) singer
a big girl	a bi(g) girl	these singers	the(se) singers
a big cake	a bi(g) cake		

Note: This type of elision can affect grammatical sequences, too.

For example, the sequence *used to* (*When I was young I used to live in Brighton*) is only pronounced /juːst tuː/ when one is speaking very, very slowly. Normally, it is pronounced /juːstə/ as if it were *use to*.

And the reduced form of *had* in a sentence such as, *I'd just got in when the phone rang*, normally becomes so much part of the following *just*, that the sequence sounds exactly like *I just got in when the phone rang*.

Elision of initial consonants in pronouns

In Part I, we talked about strong and weak forms of pronouns. Listen again to part of an earlier poem, paying particular attention to the pronunciation of the pronoun *he*.

> **4**
>
> 1 The first boy said that he'd like a slice of bread.
>
> 2 The second boy muttered that he'd really like it buttered.
>
> 3 The third boy replied that he'd rather have it fried.
>
> 4 The next boy trilled that he much preferred it grilled.
>
> 5 The last boy was quiet ... but *he* was on a diet.

What happens is that in lines 1–4 the pronoun *he* is unimportant and unstressed. So, when spoken at this speed, it loses the initial /h/ sound and becomes a simple /i/, linked to the preceding *that*.

Now listen to line 5. In this case, the pronoun *he* has its full, strong form /hiː/. This is because he, the last boy, contrasts with the other four.

> So, the pronoun *he* is found in this poem in two distinct forms:
>
> • /i/ the very **weak, unstressed** form; and
>
> • /hiː/ the **strong, stressed** form.

Other pronouns in their weakest forms may also lose their initial consonants. You can practise three of them, *her*, *him* and *them*, in the following chant, 'Have you seen Peter?'. Note that the chant also gives practice in contrasting the use of the past simple and present perfect tenses.

Compare:

past simple	present perfect
I saw him half an hour ago.	I've just seen her talking.
I saw them Tuesday morning.	I've seen him fairly frequently.
I saw her several hours ago.	I haven't seen her since Christmas.
I glimpsed him in the canteen.	I've seen her several times today.

Remember that the **past simple** is associated with specific moments in the past: *half an hour ago / Tuesday morning / (when I was) in the canteen*. The **present perfect**, by contrast, refers to an unspecified time or a time extending up to the present: *fairly frequently / since Christmas / several times today*, and may be found in the context *I've just ...*

> **5**
>
> **Have you seen Peter? (1)**
>
> 1 Have you seen Peter? Have you seen Pete?
>   I saw (h)im half an hour ago, running down the street.
>
> 2 Have you seen Patricia, have you seen Pat?
>   I've just seen (h)er talking to ᵂ(h)er little ginger cat.
>
> 3 Have you seen my neighbours, Anthony and Mark?
>   I saw (th)em Tuesday morning, strolling in the park.
>
> 4 Have you seen Samantha, have you seen Sam?
>   I saw (h)er several hours ago, eating bread and jam.
>
> 5 Have you seen Vincent, have you seen Vince?
>   I talked to ᵂ(h)im on Tuesday, but I haven't seen him since.
>
> 6 Have you seen William, have you seen Bill?
>   I may have seen (h)im yesterday, walking up the hill.

7 Have you seen Benjamin, have you seen Ben?
I've seen (h)im somewhere recently, I can't remember when.

8 Have you seen Violet, have you seen Vi?
I spoke to (h)er this morning, but I can't remember why.

9 Have you seen Matthew, have you seen Mat?
I saw (h)im talking to the Queen, so what do you think of that!

10 Have you seen Susan, have you seen Sue?
I haven'(t) seen (h)er since Christmas and I don't know what to do!

Task 26 **In the second version of the chant, the second line ends with a missing one-syllable adjective. See if you can guess the word.**

If you cannot guess, choose it from the list following the poem. As you can see from the example, more than one may be possible. (Be careful, we have put in some words that cannot fit.)

Have you seen Peter? (2)

1 Have you seen Peter, have you seen Pete?
I spotted (h)im an hour ago, looking very (neat / sweet)

2 Have you seen my parents, my mum and my dad?
I've seen (th)em several times today, looking really (.....................)

3 Have you seen Nelly, have you seen Nell?
I saw (h)er in the classroom, looking very (.....................)

4 Have you seen my parents, my dad and my mum?
I've seen (th)em once or twice today, looking pretty (.....................)

5 Have you seen Patrick, have you seen Pat?
I glimpsed (h)im in the canteen, looking very (.....................)

6 Have you seen Nicholas, have you seen Nick?
I saw (h)im in the cinema, looking slightly (.....................)

7 Have you seen my cousins, Anthony and Bart?
I noticed (th)em a while ago, looking rather (.....................)

8 Have you seen Diana, have you seen Di?
I've seen (h)er once or twice today, looking rather (.....................)

9 Have you seen Jimmy, have you seen Jim?
I saw (h)im twenty minutes back, looking very (.....................)

10 Have you seen Lynda, have you seen Lyn?
I've seen (h)er several times today, looking very (.....................)

11 Have you seen Katie, have you seen Kate?
I've seen (h)er twice this afternoon, looking really (.....................)

12 Have you seen what's-his-name, the man from number nine?
I saw (h)im down the pub last night, looking really (.....................)

13 Have you seen what's-her-name, the girl from number two?
I think I've seen (h)er recently, looking very (.....................)

blue / numb / late / grim / bad / thin / sick / hell / thick / glum / glad / high / swell / mad / flat / new / shy / fat / sad / great / fine / tart / quick / nine / smart / slim / mine / well / sly

Chapter 9
Assimilation

Assimilation of /n/

We have already come across this form of assimilation, where the nasal consonant /n/ can change to become more like the following sound. In Part I we said:

'In *and Patricia*, for example, the /d/ goes and then the /n/ becomes /m/ because of the following /p/ and we end up with /əm pə'trɪʃə/. In the same way, *and Kate* = /ən 'keit/. (The symbol /ŋ/ represents the consonant sound at the end of *song, thing, wrong*, etc.)'

We saw the same thing happening with *the secon(d) boy* and *the seco(n)d girl*.

* *secon(d) boy* became /sekəm bɔɪ/, the /d/ being elided and the /n/ changing to /m/ because of the following /b/.
* *secon(d) girl* became /sekəŋ gɜ:l/, the /d/ again going, but this time the /n/ changing to /ŋ/ because of the following /g/.

Task 27   Read the following poem aloud and see if you can work out:
* when the letter *n* in the word *ten* will still be pronounced /n/, even when read quite fast, and
* when the /n/ will change to something else.
* Then listen to the recording and see if you were right.

Ten boys and ten girls

1 Ten boys and ten girls;
   ten rubies, ten pearls.

2 Ten dogs and ten cats;
   ten coats and ten hats.

3 Ten whales and ten sharks;
   ten gardens, ten parks.

4 Ten shouts and ten sighs;
   ten truths and ten lies.

5 Ten peaches, ten grapes;
   ten monkeys, ten apes.

6 Ten brooches, ten rings;
   ten people, ten things.

7 Ten saucers, ten cups;
   ten downs and ten ups.

8 Ten dolls and ten toys;
   ten girls and ten boys.

As usual, it is a question of making things easy for the speaker. If you are going to close your lips for /b/ or /p/, then it is easier to close them for the preceding nasal. Similarly, if you are going to produce a nasal before raising the back of the tongue to the soft palate, it might as well be the nasal that belongs there anyway.

Assimilation of /d/ and /t/

In addition to /n/, the other two alveolar consonants /d/ and /t/ can also assimilate.

/d/ can become:
* /b/ (before /b/ or /p/), or
* /g/ (before /g/ or /k/), so

sequence	slow version	fast version
third boy	/θɜ:d bɔɪ/	/θɜ:b bɔɪ/
third person	/θɜ:d pɜ:sən/	/θɜ:b pɜ:sən/
third girl	/θɜ:d gɜ:l/	/θɜ:g gɜ:l/
third cat	/θɜ:d kæt/	/θɜ:g kæt/

/t/ can become:

- /p/ (before /b/ or /k/), or

- /k/ (before /g/ or /k/).

But, rather more commonly, /t/ can become a **glottal stop** before another consonant, even another /t/. For example:

sequence	slow version	fast version	or
that boy	/ðæt bɔɪ/	/ðæp bɔɪ/	/ðæʔ bɔɪ/
that person	/ðæt pɜːsən/	/ðæp pɜːsən/	/ðæʔ pɜːsən/
that girl	/ðæt gɜːl/	/ðæk gɜːl/	/ðæʔ gɜːl/
that cat	/ðæt kæt/	/ðæk kæt/	/ðæʔ kæt/
that time	/ðæt taɪm/		/ðæʔ taɪm/

Elision giving rise to assimilation

In sequences such as *ten boys and ten girls*, assimilation takes place because the sounds involved are already next to each other.

By contrast, in others such as *the second boy* and *the second girl*, assimilation only takes place because the intervening sound – the /d/ in this case – has been elided.

There are hundreds of set expressions involving this combination of /d/ or /t/ elision + assimilation.

Using 'and'

eggs an(d) bacon	/ˌegzəm ˈbeɪkən/
boys an(d) girls	/ˌbɔɪzəŋ ˈgɜːlz/
tea an(d) coffee	/ˌtiːʲəŋ ˈkɒfi/
en(d)s an(d) means	/ˌenzəm ˈmiːnz/

Negative /t/

I won('t) be coming	/aɪ ˌwəʊm bi ˈkʌmɪŋ/
She can('t) go	/ʃi ˈkɑːŋ ˈgəʊ/
Can('t) pay, won('t) pay	/ˌkɑːmpeɪ ˈwəʊmpeɪ/
I don('t) care	/aɪ ˌdəʊŋ ˈkeə/

Compounds and phrases

Here is a small selection of dozens of compounds and phrases where assimilation occurs: *lan(d) mine / ren(t) book / gran(d)mother / han(d)cuffs / han(d)bag / win(d)mill / san(d)bag / sal(t) mine / stan(d) back / corn(ed) beef / tinn(ed) beans / sal(t) beef /* etc.

And you do not have to speak at all fast for such assimilation to take place. The word *handcuffs* sounds as if it were *hangcuffs* more often than not; and your *grandmother* is usually your *grammother*.

The importance of collocation and frequency of use

> In fact, speed of delivery – the rate at which you speak – is only one factor in deciding whether elision and/or assimilation is likely to take place; there are two further factors which come into play.

The first is **collocation**. By this, we mean the frequency with which words (or other elements) are found together. Thus, the items *instant + coffee* are more likely to be found together (i.e., to **collocate**) than *fragrant + coffee* or *instant + response* for instance. Hence the /t/ in *instant coffee* is more likely to be elided than that in the two other phrases.

The second is **frequency of use**. When instant coffee was a rarity, people presumably used the phrase *instant coffee* quite carefully, unsure that other people would be familiar with the expression. But as it became more familiar, so the name became used more frequently and would be spoken with greater ease and rapidity.

Take the word *handkerchief*. It used to be composed of two separate words: *hand + kerchief*. But they became so closely associated in the compound *handkerchief* that the /d/ disappeared permanently; it is incorrect to pronounce the /d/ nowadays.

In *handbag* the /d/, by contrast, has not permanently disappeared. But you would have to be speaking very slowly and emphatically to pronounce it.

When you come to a much less common compound – *handmaid*, for example – you are much more likely to pronounce the full word, /d/ included.

So we can establish the useful principle that the more frequently two elements come together, the greater their likelihood of collocation and the more probable it is that a change will occur.

Task 28   This task is to see if you can identify elision and assimilation.

There is quite a lot of both in the following poem: 'Born and bred in London'. For example, the /t/ or /d/ of final ~ed disappears in a number of cases: listen out for:

I've jogg(ed) down ... stroll(ed) through ... saunter(ed) down ... walk(ed) the ... lurch(ed) down.

Elision and/or assimilation can also occur where two words meet in place names. *Wood Green* can become /ˌwʊg ˈgriːn/, for example, and *Green Park* /ˌgriːm ˈpɑːk/.

In this poem, there is one (and only one) example in each verse of a place name being affected by elision and/or assimilation. So:

• Read the poem to yourself and try to predict which place name in each verse is changed because of assimilation.

• Listen to it several times to see if you can hear it happening.

(Don't worry too much about the meaning of the different verbs; we'll deal with this in the next task.)

Born and bred in London

I was born and bred in London;
I know it like the back of my hand;
from Camden Lock
to the Shell-Mex clock,
from Old Street to the Strand.

I've jogged down Piccadilly
and strolled through Leicester Square,
been to Holland Park
for a ramble in the dark,
and to Hampstead for the fair.

I know every street in London;
I could do it with my eyes tight shut;
from Madame Tussauds
to the House of Lords
from Hyde Park to The Cut.

I've sauntered down to Kentish Town
and run to Tottenham Hale,
walked the Old Kent Road
while it hailed and snowed
and lurched down Maida Vale.

I know my way round London,
no-one knows it better than me;
been to Hammersmith Palais,
Covent Garden for the ballet
and The Ritz for china tea.

I visit the Bond Street Galleries,
I'm seen at the best affairs;
go to Waterloo
for a private view,
drink Pimm's on the Crush Bar stairs.

I've been everywhere in London,
by taxi, bus and train;
I've crawled, I've biked,
I've hopped, I've hiked,
from Saint Paul's to Drury Lane.

And though I've seen the lot now,
from London Bridge to Kew,
I would do it all again,
From Blackheath to old Big Ben,
just to show it all to you.

Note that names with *Street* are compounds: OLD Street, OXford Street, BOND Street, etc. All other two-part place names are phrases:

ˌOxford ˈCircus, ˌHyde ˈPark, ˌLondon ˈBridge, ˌSaint ˈPaul's, etc.

Task 29   The poem is full of verbs of movement. If necessary, use your dictionary to check the meanings, then put ticks in the appropriate columns to complete the following table.

	on hands and knees	faster than walking	on one foot	no sense of hurry	usually in the country	out of control
jog						
stroll						
ramble						
saunter						
run						
lurch						
crawl						
hop						
hike						

Task 30   **Your task this time is a dictation. All the names of things to eat or drink have been cut out. Listen to the rap as often as you want to, and fill in all the gaps bit by bit.**

This is quite fast (but no faster than regular informal speech), so watch out for elision and assimilation, especially where an ~ed may disappear between two consonants.

A diner is a type of restaurant best-known in the USA. (You may have seen them in films from the 1950s and 1960s.) They usually have a long counter with a row of single stools, and a few booths for four people from where you can choose music from the jukebox. I wrote this rap after eating in a genuine restored original diner here in London.

Down the diner

I was sitting down the diner, toying with my food,
looking at the papers, in a lazy kind of mood

when a little skinny fellow I'd never seen before
came and sat down beside me, and this is what I saw:

my favourite waitress, Sally, came over to the guy
to ask him for his order, and this was his reply:

'I'd like a (1) ...., make sure it's really hot,
and a (2) .... should really hit the spot,

with a (3) .... and a touch of (4) ....
then a (5) .... with some (6) .... and (7) ....,

and a (8) .... or two of (9) .... with some (10) ....
then a (11) ...., with some (12) .... of course.

Can I have the (13) .... in a (14) ....?
and a good thick (15) .... well-done;

and how about some (16) ...., I like them lightly fried,
with a little piccalilli and some (17) .... on the side

and I'd like to try a couple of your (18) .... pies
with a pile of (19) .... and a plate of (20) ....

then a (21) .... – cut it really thick,
with a little (22) ...., now that should do the trick.

For dessert, I think I'll start with a good old (23) ....
with several (24) .... of (25) ...., pile 'em really high;

then a (26) .... of little (27) .... with some (28) ....
on top and an (29) ....; perhaps I'd better stop.

No, maybe there's some (30) .... that you can recommend?
OK I'll take the (31) .... and that'll be the end.'

So Sally took the order though she thought it was a joke,
then the fellow called her back and said,

'I'd like (32) ....'

Task 31   Work out which of the following will involve elision and/or assimilation

Below is another poem full of examples of assimilation and elision, 'Cash flow problems' below. Don't listen to it yet. Just see if you can guess which of the following words and phrases will involve elision and/or assimilation.

best friend	another friend	twenty pounds
landlord	sandwiches	one editor
another one	next door	brand-new
beef hash	a third one	second-hand

Task 32   Now listen to the poem and see if you can note down every example of elision and assimilation.

> **Vocabulary notes**
> a fortnight *back* = 'a fortnight ago/two weeks ago'; *corned beef* is a type of tinned beef; *dosh* is a slang word for 'cash', 'money'; a *hash* is usually made with meat and potatoes all mixed together and cooked; *mack* is short for *mackintosh* = 'raincoat' (note: a 'Mac' is an Apple Macintosh computer); to *sneak away* is to leave quietly so that nobody can see you leaving; *tosh* means 'nonsense', 'rubbish', 'of no value'.

113

3/4

Cash flow problems

My best friend bought me
a brand-new handbag;
another friend bought me
a second-hand mack;
My next-door neighbour
said he'd lend me
twenty pounds till Monday,
    The problem is
        I don't know how
            I'm going to pay them back!

My landlord brought me
some roast beef sandwiches;
my landlady made me
some corned beef hash;
my grandmother sent me
a case of canned potatoes.
    The problem is
        I don't know where
            I'm going to get the cash!

One editor said that
she rather liked a poem;
another one said that
they were a load of tosh;
a third one said that
they might use one at Christmas.
    The problem is
        it's right now
          I really need
            the dosh!

A fortnight back I told them all
I'd come up with the money.
Last week I promised that
I'd really, truly pay.
If I haven't got it next week
there's only one thing for it.
    I'd better get
        my bags
          all packed
            and quietly
              sneak
                away.

Coalescent assimilation

/d/ or /t/ + /j/

The last poem 'Cash flow problems' contained the line *they might use one at Christmas*. Spoken slowly and carefully this would be:

/ðeɪ maɪt juːz wʌn ət krɪsməs/

But *might* ends with a /t/ and *use* begins with a /j/. And the sound /j/ tends to combine with a preceding /d/ or /t/. The formula is:

- /t/ + /j/ may coalesce to become /tʃ/ (= the first sound in *child*, *Charles*, etc.);
- /d/ + /j/ may coalesce to become /dʒ/ (= the first sound in *jam*, *Jane*, etc.).

So the sequence *might use*, at normal fast speed will sound like *my choose*.

This type of assimilation is particularly important because it involves some combinations of words which are so common that coalescence happens extremely frequently in ordinary speech.

/t/ + /j/

An extremely common context for /t/ to meet /j/ is when the short version of *not* is followed by *you* or *your*.

sequence	slow version	fast version
can't you?	/kɑːnt juː/	/kɑːntʃə/
won't you?	/wəʊnt juː/	/wəʊntʃə/
don't you?	/dəʊnt juː/	/dəʊntʃə/
Can't you come?	/kɑːnt juː kʌm/	/kɑːntʃə kʌm/
didn't you?	/dɪdnt juː/	/dɪdntʃə/
Didn't your (mother do it?)	/dɪdnt jɔː/	/dɪdntʃə/
wouldn't you?	/wʊdnt juː/	/wʊdntʃə/
Wouldn't your (friends help?)	/wʊdnt jɔː/	/wʊdntʃə/

Another context is when a stressed verb ending in /t/ is followed by *you* or *your*.

I bet you can't do it.	/aɪ ˈbetʃə kɑːn ˈduː ʷɪt/
I'll **meet your** friend tomorrow.	/aɪl ˈmiːtʃə ˈfren təˈmɒrəʊ/
I can't **let you** do it.[1]	/aɪ ˈkɑːn letʃə ˈduː ʷɪt/
I'll **treat your** friends (to the cinema).	/aɪl ˈtriːtʃə ˈfrenz/
I **admit you** were right.	/aɪ ədˈmɪtʃə wə ˈraɪt/

Similar coalescence can take place when the sound /t/, functioning as the ~*ed* suffix, is followed by *you* or *your*. For example:

I picked your book up.	/aɪ ˈpɪktʃə ˈbʊ kʌp/
We stopped you from doing it.	/wi ˈstɒptʃə frəm ˈdəʊɪŋ ɪt/

> **Note** that this form of assimilation can take place even with stressed *you* or *your*. So, *Don't YOU want it?* can sound like *Don('t) CHEW want it?*

---

1 Note that *let you* and *let your* sounds the same as *lecher* when spoken fast; and *picked you* / *picked your* sounds like *picture*.

/d/ + /j/

Auxiliary or modal verbs + *you*

Probably the most frequent cause of /d/ + /j/ assimilation is when certain auxiliary or modal verbs meet *you*. These are not only those verbs – *did, could* and *would* – that always end in /d/, but also the weakest form of *do*, where the vowel disappears completely.

At this point, we need to mention again that there are not always just two possibilities – a slow version and a fast one. Listen to three versions of the following four sequences.

a) Do you like jazz?
   slow   = /duː juː 'laɪk 'dʒæz/
   fast   = /dʊ jʊ 'laɪk 'dʒæz/
   very fast = /dʒə 'laɪk 'dʒæz/

b) Did you like the music?
   slow   = /dɪd juː 'laɪk ðə 'mjuːzik/
   fast   = /dɪdʒə 'laɪk ðə 'mjuːzik/
   very fast = /dʒə 'laɪk ðə 'mjuːzik/

c) Would you like to go again?
   slow   = /wʊd juː 'laɪk tə 'gəʊ ə'gen/
   fast   = /wʊdʒə 'laɪk tə 'gəʊ ə'gen/
   very fast = /dʒə 'laɪk tə 'gəʊ ə'gen/

d) Did you have a good time?
   slow   = /dɪd juː 'hæv ə 'gʊd 'taɪm/
   fast   = /dɪd 'jæv ə 'gʊd 'taɪm/
   very fast = /ˌdʒəæv 'gʊd 'taɪm/

Note: In very fast casual speech there need be no difference at all between *do you, did you* and *would you;* they can all be pronounced /dʒə/. How we can tell the difference? The context always makes it clear.

Listen to the following questions and answers, which also show the difference between the weakest and strongest forms of the auxiliaries.

Do you like jazz?	Yes, I do.
/dʒə 'laɪk 'dʒæz/	/je saɪ 'duː/
Did you like the music last night?	Yes, I did.
/dʒə 'laɪk ðə 'mjuːzik 'lɑːs 'naɪt/	/je saɪ 'dɪd/
Would you like to go again?	Yes, I would.
/dʒə 'laɪk tə 'gəʊ ə'gen/	/je saɪ 'wʊd/

Verbs ending in /d/ followed by *you/your*

I've **made** your bed.	/aɪv 'meɪdʒə 'bed/
Have you **paid** your bill?	/həv jə 'peɪdʒə 'bɪl/
I **said you** should come.	/aɪ 'sedʒə ʃʊg 'kʌm/

Note that, as with /t/, the assimilation can take place even with the stressed forms of *you* and *your*.

~ed

I **mentioned your** name.	/aɪ ˈmenʃəndʒə ˈneɪm/
I **wanted you** to come.	/aɪ ˈwʌntɪdʒə tə ˈkʌm/
They **said you** shouldn('t) do it.	/ðeɪ ˈsedʒʊ ˈʃʊdn ˈduː ʷɪt/

Now practice this form of assimilation by listening to and repeating the 'Chinatown' rap on pages 66–67. The lefthand column shows how it is pronounced, with the letter *a* representing schwa.

normal form	written here	phonetic notation
want to	wanna	/ˈwʌnə/
going to	gointa	/ˈɡəʊintə/
do you	dja	/dʒə/
what do you	whatcha	/ˈwɒtʃə/
don't you	dontcha	/ˈdəʊntʃə/
let you	letcha	/ˈletʃə/
couldn't you	couldntcha	/ˈkʊdntʃə/
have to	hafta[2]	/ˈhæftə/
did you	didja	/ˈdɪdʒə/
how did you	howdja	/ˈhaʊdʒə/
where do you	wheredja	/ˈweədʒə/
lots of	lotsa	/ˈlɒtsə/
the name of	the namea	/ðə ˈneɪmə/
a bit of	a bit a	/ə ˈbɪtə/
sure to	sure ta	/ˈʃɔːtə/

Other features of fast speech are also reflected in the changes of spelling. Look out for the following.

elision or lengthening of identical/similar sounds

normal form	written here
I'm not too sure	I'm no' too sure
I'll leave it to you	I' leave it to you
I'll let you know	I' letcha know
It's sure to please	It' sure ta please

elision of /t/

normal form	written here
Let's just meet	Le's just meet
didn't say	didn' say
I don't know	I don' know
it wasn't written	it wasn' written

Don't get so carried away by the rhythm that you read the rap like a machine. Remember that language has music, too.

2   This spelling of *have to* shows how, at speed, the /v/ of *have* can become /f/, losing its voicing to be more like the following /t/ sound.

Rhymes and Rhythm

Listen, listen, listen, many, many times, thinking how the voice goes up and down. DAH du DAH it before you say the words. And when you finally rap it along with the recording, follow the voices up and down.

Don't forget that the pitch changes (how we go from high to low, from low to high) are smooooooooth on the stressed syllables. Take the title word, *Chinatown*. We don't say it in three equal stages, as if it were:

Chi

    na

       town

Instead, there is a nice smooth, steady fall on *Chi*, with the next two syllables safe at the bottom of the voice, not moving. So think of it as:

C h
  i
   i
    i
     n a t o w n

Finally, remember that this is a conversation. It may sound fast, but it is no faster than regular, informal speech.

But don't think you have to repeat it all at once. You can practice a sequence in short bits, starting from the end to keep the intonation going. Try it with the following sentences.

1 a show?
see a show?
ta see a show?
ta town ta see a show?
go ta town ta see a show?
wanna go ta town ta see a show?
Doncha wanna go ta town ta see a show?

2 Chinatown?
in Chinatown?
first in Chinatown?
fancy eating first in Chinatown?
Dja fancy eating first in Chinatown?

Chinatown

2/3

How it sounds	How it is written
A: **Where** dja wanna go? **Whatcha** wanna do?	Where do you want to go? What do you want to do?
B: I'm **no'** too sure, I' **leave** it ta you.	I'm not too sure, I'll leave it to you.
A: **Doncha** wanna go ta town ta **see** a show?	Don't you want to go to town to see a show?
B: I **don'** know now, but l' **letcha** know.	I don't know now, but I'll let you know.
A: **Couldn**tcha tell me **right** away?	Couldn't you tell me right away?
B: I'm **not** sure yet. Do I **haf**ta say?	I'm not sure yet. Do I have to say?
A: **Where** dja wanna meet? Wontcha **tell** me where?	Where do you want to meet? Won't you tell me where?
B: **Le's** jus' meet in **Leicester** Square.	Let's just meet in Leicester Square.

A: **Did**ja tell the others
where we're **goin**ta meet?

B: I **said** in the centre,
didn' **say** which street.

A: Dja **wan**na have a meal or
dja **like** ta sit down?

B: Dja **fan**cy eating first
in **China**town?

A: **What**cha recommend?
Wheredja **like** ta dine?

B: **Here's** very good,
their **fish** is fine.

A: **How's** the fish cooked,
with **lotsa** spice?

B: **Just** a bit a ginger,
it's **really** nice.

A: **What**cha like ta drink
when you **eat** Chinese?

B: **Just** a pot a tea,
it' **sure** ta please.

A: **How**dja like the meal,
Didja **like** the fish?

B: It was **really** great,
what's the **name**a the dish?

A: I **don'** know the name;
it **wasn'** written down.

B: That's **often** the way
... in **China**town.

Did you tell the others
where we're going to meet?

I said in the centre,
didn't say which street.

Do you want to have a meal or
would you like to sit down?

Do you fancy eating first
in Chinatown?

What do you recommend?
Where would you like to dine?

Here's very good,
their fish is fine.

How's the fish cooked,
with lots of spice?

Just a bit of ginger,
it's really nice.

What do you like to drink
when you eat Chinese?

Just a pot of tea,
it's sure to please.

How did you like the meal?
did you like the fish?

It was really great,
what's the name of the dish?

I don't know the name;
it wasn't written down.

That's often the way
... in Chinatown.

/s/ or /z/ + /j/

The fricatives /s/ and /z/ can also coalesce with /j/.

*   /s/ + /j/ → /ʃ/ (as in *shop, she, ship, dish*, etc.).

*   /z/ + /j/ → /ʒ/ (as in *pleasure, television, camouflage*, etc.)

sequence	slow version	fast version
Is this yours?	/ɪz ðɪs ˈjɔːz/	/ɪz ðɪ ˈʃɔːz/
Yes, you can.	/jes juː ˈkæn/	/jeʃə ˈkæn/
He's your brother.	/hiːz jɔː ˈbrʌðə/	/hiːʒə ˈbrʌðə/
Are these yours?	/ɑː ðiːz ˈjɔːz/	/ɑː ðiː ˈʒɔːz/

Task 33 **Listen to the chant on this page while reading the text. Pay special attention to what happens to the /j/ sound in *you, your* and *yourself* when the teacher replies.**

Here are the words that come before *you, your* and *yourself*. Each ends in either /ʃ/ or /ʒ/. Tick the appropriate column.

	/ʃ/	/ʒ/		/ʃ/	/ʒ/
course			please		
discuss			express		
miss			revise		
use			pass		
practise			amaze		

Can I ask you something?

Student	**Teacher**
1 Can I ask you something?	Of course you can.
2 It's all so hard.	Let's discuss your problems.
3 I'm falling behind.	Don't miss your lessons.
4 I don't understand.	Well, use your head.
5 My accent's bad.	Well, practise your pron.
6 Should I listen to some tapes?	Please yourself.
7 I don't know what to write.	Just express yourself.
8 I make lots of mistakes.	Revise your grammar.
9 How d'you think I'll do?	You're sure to pass your exam.
10 Do you really think I will?	You'll amaze your friends.

Rapping the rules

These first three Parts have covered the main features of spoken English, in terms of rhythm and stress. These are summarized in a set of five rules, which I've written as a rap.

1 You have to stress the correct syllables. And the weak syllables must **never** be too long. The schwa, in particular, is very short. Remember that placing main stress in the wrong place can cause people not to understand you.

2 To keep the rhythm flowing along you have to link individual words. Remember:

one napple, two wapples, three yapples, four rapples

3 And it's much easier if you elide the sounds that native speakers do, especially the /d/ and /t/ between consonants.

4 Natural speech also means that we can make it easier to pass from one sound to the next by changing the first to be more like the second (i.e., anticipatory assimilation).

5 Finally, two sounds may join together to become one, especially when /d/, /t/, /s/ and /ʃ/ meets /j/ (i.e., coalescent assimilation).

If you **want** to make your English **come alive,**
just **listen** to my **rules** from **one** to **five.**

1 If you **don't** want your English to **sound** a **mess,**
   you've **got** to hit the **beat,** you've **got** to hit the **stress.**
   But you're **going** to sound **funny,** it's **going** to go **wrong**
   if you **make** your **weak** sounds **much** too **strong.**

2 And **words** go together like **links** in a **chain;**
   they **follow** each **other** like **wagons** on a **train.**

3 Now **listen** really **close** and **you** will **hear**
   that **certain** kinds of **sound** can **disappear.**

4 And **remem**ber if you **want** to increase your **range**
   that a **sound** can **make** ano**ther** sound change.

5 You're **getting** better **now,** but to **be** the **best,**
   just **remem**ber two **sounds** can coalesce.

You've **got** five **senses,** you've **got** five **rules,**
so **use** them **all** and you **won't** be **fools.**
So, to **make** your English **buzz** like a **hive,**
just **think** of **one, two, three, four, FIVE!**

Task 34 Listen to the rap again very carefully in order to see how the rules apply when you speak at this speed.

This last task is like a final examination to see how good your ear has become. (And remember this: the rap might sound fast, but it's no faster than regular, informal spoken English.)

So go through the text and note:

a) every example of **linking** in Verse 2;

b) every example of **elision** in the introduction and Verse 5;

c) every example of **anticipatory assimilation** in Verses 3, 4 and 5;

d) every example of **coalescent assimilation** in the whole rap.

In these first three parts you have learned a lot about what happens in spoken English.

The rest of the book is to help you put your new skills into practice.

PART IV Playing with poems

Part IV presents a number of poems that have been chosen for two reasons:

- to give you practice in the rhythm of spoken English;
- to improve and increase your vocabulary.

The tasks in this unit are of various types. Most involve filling gaps with appropriate words, in others you will have to match parts of sentences, do some rewriting, and so on.

All the limericks have been recorded, so you can listen to the recordings to help you during the task or after completing it.

Whatever the task, remember that the choice of words depends on two things: first, the meaning; obviously, a word has to make sense, to fit into the rest of the text; but as these texts are poems, it also has to fit the **metre** (i.e., the beat, the rhythm) and, if the word is at the end of a line, it has to fit the **rhyme scheme** too.

Feel free to listen to the poems before trying the tasks, if you feel happier. And if you are wondering which word fits a gap, try the DAH du du technique; this will help you to work out if you need a word with one syllable, or two or three. If it is a two-syllable word, it will help you decide if the pattern is ○■ or ■○, for example.

Remember, once more, not to worry too much if you do not fully understand all the words. Concentrate on the rhythm and music; imagine the words flowing by like waves on the sea and follow them along, with all their up and down movements. Poems are to be enjoyed, not to be worried about.

Chapter 10
Limericks

What are limericks?

Limericks are very simple poems. Listen to the following, very typical one.

> A: There once was a person from Lyme
> A: who married three wives at a time.
> B: When asked 'Why a third?'
> B: He replied, 'One's absurd!
> A: And bigamy, sir, is a crime!'

Limericks have the following characteristics:

- They consist of **five lines**.
- The **rhyme scheme** is A A B B A.

  This means that lines 1, 2 and 5 have one rhyme (in the case above *Lyme / time / crime*), while lines 3 and 4 have a different rhyme (*third / absurd*).
- The **metre** (or beat) is as regular as the rhyme scheme: three beats in the A lines, and two in the B lines.

Note also that the first line refers to a person from a particular place. This is not obligatory, but many limericks have a similar reference in the first line.

Listen again while beating it out.

>   a   ONE   and a TWO   and a   THREE
> A: There once was a person from Lyme
>   a   ONE   and a   TWO and a THREE
> A: who married three wives at a time.
>   a   ONE   and a   TWO
> B: When asked 'Why a third?'
>   a   ONE   and a   TWO
> B: He replied, 'One's absurd!
>   a ONE and a TWO and a THREE
> A: And bigamy, sir is a crime!'

When doing the tasks in this section, it is a good idea to have a good dictionary handy, so that you can check the rhymes (as well as the meanings).

Gap-fill tasks

Task 35   The rhyming words in the following limerick have been jumbled together at the end. Fill them in as quickly as you can.

> 1 There once was an old man from ...
> 2 who dreamed he was eating his ...
> 3 He woke up in the ...
> 4 with a terrible ...
> 5 and found it was perfectly ...
> ───────────
> fright / shoe / true / night / Crewe

Task 36   Here are two limericks on the theme of music, with their rhyming words jumbled up at the end. Again, fill them as quickly as possible.

1 A musician who came from Hong ...
2 Composed a new popular ...
3 But the song that he ...
4 Was all on one ...
5 Though it sounded superb on a ...

6 A musical girl called ...
7 Played 'God Save the Queen' on a ...
8 Or so she ...
9 But people who ...
10 Were never quite able to ...

tell / wrote / Kong / heard / song / Estelle / averred (= said, stated, claimed) / bell / gong / note

Task 37   And now we go up to three limericks with the rhyming words left out and jumbled up. And this time an extra word has been added for each rhyme, to confuse things.

1 A diner while dining at ...
2 Found a rather large mouse in his ...
3 Said the waiter, 'Don't ...
4 And wave it ...
5 Or the rest will be wanting one ...!'

6 A glutton who came from the ...,
7 When asked at what hour he would ...,
8 Replied, 'At ...,
9 At three, five and ...,
10 And eight and a quarter past ...'.

11 There was an old lady of ...
12 Whose nose was remarkably ...
13 One day, they ...,
14 She followed her ...,
15 For no-one knows which way she ...

about / bent (= not straight) / chew / Crewe / dine / eleven / grows / heaven / Kent / nine / nose / Rhine / sent / seven / shout / out / stew (= a dish cooked slowly in water) / suppose / too / wine / went

Correcting tasks

In the following tasks, you will have to correct mistakes in a number of limericks. In some, the lines are jumbled together, in others, there is something wrong with the rhyme scheme or metre.

Task 38   **This time we have mixed three limericks together. Only lines 1 and 3 are in the correct place in each limerick.**

1 There was a young girl in the choir
  Used language I dare not pronounce.
3 Till it reached such a height
  Pulled her chair out behind
  For careless old people like you!'

6 A girl who weighed many an ounce
  Once dropped her false teeth in the stew.
8 For a fellow, unkind,
  'It's horrid to cater
  And they found it next day in the spire.

11 A certain old lady from Crewe
  Whose voice rose up higher and higher
13 Said a sensitive waiter
  It was clear out of sight
  Just to see (so he said) if she'd bounce.

Vocabulary notes
to *bounce* is what happens to a rubber ball, for example, when you drop it on the floor; to *cater* = either 'look after' or 'provide food for': a *choir* (pronounced /kwaɪə/) is a group of people who sing together; an *ounce* is a small unit of weight, so 'weighed many an ounce' = 'was very fat'; *sensitive*, here, = 'easily hurt, easily upset'; a *spire* is a thin tower on top of a church; *stew* was explained in the last task.

Task 39   **In the following limericks, the lines in bold have the correct rhymes, but something has gone wrong with the others. Suggest correct rhymes for them. (If you find this too difficult, choose the words from the list after the limericks.)**

1 **A sprightly old man from LA**
2 Once said to his wife, 'If I might,
3 I think I will walk
4 **On my head in the Strand,'**
5 To which she retorted: 'Why not.'

6 **A greedy old grandad from Duns,**
7 Once said he'd eat ninety-nine cakes.
8 At the seventy-ninth,
9 **He unluckily burst,**
10 So the rest were consumed by his boss.

---

stand / okay / buns / first / may / sons

Task 40   **This time the rhymes are all fine, but something has gone wrong with the metre, except in one line per poem, printed in bold. Some words are too long, others too short; or there are too many or too few words.**

* See if you can work out what is wrong.

* Then look at the list of words which you will need to use.

* And if that is still too difficult, listen to the recording to hear what needs changing.

> **Vocabulary notes**
> **1ˢᵗ limerick:** *an acquaintance* is someone you know, but not very well; *tame* is the opposite of *wild* (dogs are tame, but lions are usually wild).
>
> **2ⁿᵈ limerick:** a *greedy* person is someone who eats a lot; *gherkins* = pickled cucumbers; to *pickle* = 'to preserve food – vegetables usually – in vinegar or salt water'; *internal workings*, in this poem, means 'the inside of her body'.
>
> **3ʳᵈ limerick:** a *blaze* is a strongly burning fire; *charred* means 'burned black on the outside'; to *glow* = 'to burn gently, but brightly'.

awfully / could not / fear / friends / fuel / her / heightened / man / remind / started / terribly / threw / young

---

There was an old gentleman of Khartoum
Who kept two tame sheep in his room.
To make him think, he said
Of two acquaintances of his who were dead;
But he was completely unable to remember of whom.

A greedy lady called Perkins
Was fond of small gherkins.
She devoured forty-three
One day for tea
And pickled all of her internal workings.

When the shortage of things to burn made it hard,
To maintain the big blaze in our yard;
We decided to throw on Aunt Flo,
Who began to glow,
And ended up very charred.

Here is a well-known limerick which breaks the rules of both rhyme and metre. Why it does so should be obvious.

Two poets from Lytham,
Had simply no sense of rhythm.
Their limericks would rhyme
Only occasionally
So the editor sadly rejected all their work
And off they went taking their poems with 'em.

Limericks demonstrating aspects of fast speech

Weak forms of grammatical items

The last limerick contained the rhymes *Lytham / rhythm / with 'em*. It only functions as a rhyme if you use the weakest form of the pronoun *them*. The following poems all use weak forms of pronouns or of other grammatical items dealt with earlier in the book.

The most common pronoun used this way is the weakest form of *them*, pronounced /əm/. This is because it provides a rhyme for place names ending in *~ham* which, as you may remember from Part I, is also pronounced /əm/.

> **Vocabulary notes**
> *brand-new* = 'completely new'; a *quid* = 'a pound'; a *thrifty* person is very careful with money; a *vicar* is a minister of religion.

Said a man to his wife down in Sydenham,
'My trousers – now where have you hidden 'em? (= them)
It's perfectly true
That they're far from brand-new
But I foolishly left half a quid in 'em!'

A thrifty young fellow of Shoreham
Made brown paper trousers and wore 'em;
He looked nice and neat
Till he bent in the street
To pick up a pin; then he tore 'em.

There was a young lady of Twickenham
Whose shoes were too tight to walk quick in 'em.
She came back from a walk
Looking whiter than chalk
And took 'em both off and was sick in 'em.

And remember that ~ster at the end of place names also contains schwa, which means it can rhyme with the weakest form of the pronoun *her*.

There was a young lady from Gloucester
Whose parents thought that they had lost 'er (= her)
From the fridge came a sound
And at last she was found;
The trouble was how to defrost 'er.

The possessive adjective *her* also weakens to schwa in its shortest form.

There was a young lady of Ryde
Who ate some green apples and died.
The apples fermented (= became alcohol)
Inside the lamented, (= the dead person)
And made cider inside 'er inside. (= inside her inside)
= əm meid 'saɪdər ɪn 'saɪdər ɪn 'saɪd

Finally, here's a rhyme that only works if two sounds are elided.

There was a young fellow named Sydney
Who drank till he ruined his kidney.
It shrivelled and shrank
As he sat there and drank.
But he had a good time at it, didn'(t) (h)e?

To end the section on limericks, here is something I wrote just to demonstrate that it is possible to produce a poem, each stanza of which is a limerick.

'So you think you've got problems!'

There's really no problem with lexis,
it's easy whatever your sex is.
The words are the same
from sleepy old Thame
right over to Galveston, Texas.

And syntax should cause you no pain,
there's no need for worry or strain.
They use the same pattern
from Leeds to Manhattan,
from southern New Zealand to Maine.

But 'pron' is a different matter;
the brightest of brains it can shatter.
You start off confused,
aggrieved and bemused,
and end up as mad as a hatter.

A student of mine from Algiers
would frequently burst into tears,
for her rhythm and stress
were a terrible mess
and yet she'd been studying for years.

Another from Lima (Peru)
said 'Teacher, just what should I do?
Does "cough" rhyme with "rough"
and "bough" with "enough",
and what about "thorough" and "through"?'

Another young student from Spain
said 'Teacher, please could you explain
why "bury" and "ban"
and "very" and "van"
are different? To me they're the same!!'

'That's easy', said Tanaka-san,
(a nice, unassuming young man)
'but "red", "right" and "wrong"
and "led", "light" and "long"
are problems to us from Japan.'

An obstinate student from Spa
refused to acknowledge the schwa.
He said 'go **to** town'
and 'jump up **and** down'.
That's taking things rather too far!

So students and teachers all sigh,
they jibber and shiver and cry,
tearing hair from their heads,
sobbing late in their beds,
they wonder if succour is nigh.

But don't worry, help is in sight.
I'm really aware of your plight.
Just taking a look
at my latest book
will help you (at least it just might)

Chapter 11
Other types of poem

'Going shopping'

Start off by listening to the poem without looking at the text. It has a rather complicated rhyming scheme: A A B C C B. In other words, you have: a rhyming couplet followed by an non-rhyming third line, then a second rhyming couplet followed by the final line, which rhymes with the third. Pay attention to the metre as well; the scheme carries over six lines and goes like this:

	ONE	TWO	(THREE)
A: Every	time she goes out	shopping	
A: Mary	Williams drives a	whopping	
B: great big	lorry just to	carry all she	buys (pause, pause)
C: For her	family's so	large	
C: that she	really needs a	barge	
B: (there are	twenty-four of	ev(e)ry shape	and size).

So there are two main beats in the A and C lines, with three in the B lines. Pay close attention to the beat or you will try to fit in words that match the meaning but not the metre.

And when you read the poem aloud, remember what you have learned from earlier in the book. The unstressed grammatical words *and* and *of* must be very short, or you will not keep to the beat. So careful with *bread an(d) jam an(d) honey; jump an(d) cheer an(d) shout* and a *sack of macaroni*, for example.

But please don't read it like a machine. Think of the meaning. Listen to the way the voice goes up and down. And don't think that the end of a line always means the end of a grammatical unit. Sometimes it does as in:

Every time she goes out shopping.

But not in:

Mary Williams drives a whopping.

Mary Williams doesn't drive a '*whopping*'; she drives a *whopping great big lorry* (= a very big lorry). You should read lines 1–3 like this:

Every time she goes out shopping

Mary Williams drives a whopping great big lorry just to carry all she buys.

> **Vocabulary notes**
> a *barge* is a long, flat boat for carrying goods on a river or canal; *boloney* is a type of sausage (originally from *Bologna*, in Italy); *mutton* is meat from sheep; *tradesmen* are people who own shops (*tradespeople* wouldn't fit the metre); *whopping great big* means *extremely big*.

Task 41   Choose from the words below to complete gaps 1–10 in the following poem.

Only one will work at the end of lines, but there may be more than one option mid-line. Try out the DAH du du system to see if a word fits the metre as well as the meaning.

> age / all / bag / big / bit / bus / can / car / cash / cat / city / clap / confetti / dog / down / each / every / gets / hat / height / jump / money / packet / pound / sack / shout / spaghetti / tin / town / truck / up / village / wave

Task 42   Now complete gaps 11–22. This time, see how quickly you can spot the possibilities.

There are three words for each gap. Sometimes only one fits, sometimes two, sometimes all three.

who	jeans	Charley	must	sugar	time
they	beans	Peter	can	chocolate	cash
he	means	Sally	does	biscuits	money
bread	meeting	wheat	kilo	yoghurt	crates
cake	heating	meat	pound	cream	pounds
coke	baking	meet	tin	cheese	bags

Every time she goes out shopping
Mary Williams drives a whopping
great big lorry just to carry all she buys.

For her family's so large
that she really needs a barge
(there are twenty-four of every shape and size).

As she drives her lorry (1) ....
to the centre of the (2) ....
all the tradesmen start to (3) .... and cheer and (4) ....

For she spends vast sums of (5) ....
just on bread and jam and honey
(not to mention all the wine and beer and stout).

And (6) .... day she buys (7) ....
(that's for Margaret, Fred and Betty)
and some mutton chops with very little fat.

And a metre of baloney
with a (8) .... of macaroni
and a (9) .... of something tasty for the (10) ....

Then there's artichokes and (11) ....
and a case of tinned sardines,
with some anchovies and cabbages and steak.

And especially for (12) ....
(as he likes things slightly sweeter)
lots of (13) .... and a slice or two of (14) ....

She buys mustard by the (15) ....,
salt and pepper (freshly ground)
and vast quantities of butter, milk and (16) ....,

And for Cathy, Joe and Reg
(17) (... eat nothing else but veg)
several **(18)** .... of carrots, radishes and peas.

As for her, what **(19)** .... she eat,
is it fish or fruit or **(20)** ....?
What's the kind of thing that mothers like the best?

Well she's got no **(21)** .... for eating
for she's cooking or she's **(22)** ....
up the food she's bought to serve to all the rest.

'Song for London'

This poem/song, with its simple A B C B rhyming scheme, sums up the way I feel about London. Yes, it's noisy, polluted, dirty and sometimes dangerous; but it's also one of the most exciting cities in the world, with lively street markets, greenery and water, and just about the best theatre, art and music scenes you will find anywhere, with a population from all over the world.

You can work on this poem in different ways:

a) Just read it and try to guess what the missing words are. (Usually, just one word is missing, but gaps 4, 19, 22, 29 and 35 contain three words each, so you could leave these to last.)

b) Look at the following word lists and choose the ones that fit.

c) Use it as a dictation, by listening to the poem and filling the gaps.

But take care if you try methods a or b. Some words may fit the **meaning** but not the **metre**. So say a line out loud, with a du DAH or a DAH duh duh, and so on, to replace the missing word. Ask yourself, 'is there one syllable missing here? Two? Three?' Then try out the word you think best fits.

Pre-task and vocabulary notes
Brick Lane and *Camden Town* have lively markets at the weekend;
Dr Samuel Johnson was an 18th-century writer, best known for his dictionary;
to *choke* = usually 'not to be able to breathe';
to *glint* = 'to shine when the light catches an object, a ring, for example';
to *hurtle* = 'to move very fast, usually past something else';
to *lurk* = 'to hide in wait for someone, perhaps to attack them';
to *mess up* = 'to make something dirty or untidy';
potholes are very big holes in roads, especially dangerous for cyclists like me;
a *spyhole* is a little glass-covered hole in a door, so you can see who a visitor is but they can't see you;
trash = *rubbish*: 'things thrown away'.

Task 43   Choose from the words below to complete the following poem. Sometimes more than one can fit a gap. Gaps 4, 19, 22, 29 and 35 will be completed in Task 44.

Part A

glad	rising	weather	tubes	fog	at
arrows	shining	explain	for	rainbows	smog
pleased	dirt	by	happy	agree	fumes
buses	trains	diamonds	setting	gold	

Part B

in	use	speak	die	film	scared
darkness	know	drive	play	after	lorries
cry	buses	concert	afraid	midnight	dark
pub	cycle	nightfall	for	look	cars
frightened					

Part C

cats	walk	traffic	decide	put	trash
helicopters	dogs	night	agree	but	rubbish
up	take	down	sleeping	stroll	though
cycle	pollution	dark	breathing	get	

Task 44   Now sort out the following words to fill gaps 4, 19, 22, 29 and 35.

at	at	of	to	why	the
you	care	leave	tell	seems	eight
tired	door	life			

_____

A The roads are full of potholes
and the streets are full of trash,
the pavements lined with youngsters
asking, 'can you spare some cash?'

The (1) .... are packed to bursting
and the (2) .... always late.
If you want to get to town (3) .... noon
you'd better (4) _____

But when the sun is (5) ....
and the river glints like (6) ....,
and the bridges curve like (7) ....,
then the city takes its hold.

And I'm (8) .... to be in London,
though I really can't (9) ....
And London's where I live,
despite the (10) ...., the (11) .... and rain.

B The (12) .... hurtle past me
as I (13) .... to my work.
If I come home after (14) ....
I'm (15) .... of who might lurk.

You hardly (16) .... your neighbours
(17) .... 20 years or more,
and (18) .... a little spyhole
when someone's (19) _____.

But when I'm sitting waiting
for the (20) .... to begin,
or a (21) .... by some young writer
makes me think that we might win,

then I'm glad to be in London,
though it's hard to (22) _____.
And London is the city
where I'll live until I (23) ....

C   The (24) .... mess up the pavement,
the kids daren't use the park;
the traffic wrecks the daytime;
alarms disturb the (25) ....

The (26) .... chokes the gutters,
(27) .... fills the air,
old folks have trouble (28) ....
and no-one (29) _____.

But when I (30) .... at weekends
through Brick Lane or Camden Town,
I realize that, though
there's plenty here to (31) .... me (32) ....

I (33) .... with Doctor Johnson
(34) (... I can't speak for my wife)
that a man who's tired of London
is a man who's (35) _____.

'Failure'

Vocabulary notes
when the stock market *crashes*, the value of shares goes down;
a *fake* is something (usually a work of art) that is a copy of the original, used to deceive;
a *pheasant* is a game bird, i.e., a bird bred for shooting and eating;
to *pot* – 'to hit a ball into the pocket' when playing billiards or snooker. If you aim for one colour and hit another you lose points;
to be given the *sack* is to be fired, to lose your job;
tame is the opposite of *wild*;
a *wren* is a small song-bird.

Task 45   **This is another poem in rhyming couplets. As you can see from the first couplet, it is about a man for whom everything goes wrong.**

Something has gone wrong with the poem, too. Your task is to match the endings to the beginnings of each line.

3/4

He studied so hard but the others all passed.
He tried to be first but he always came last.

1 He learned Japanese	a)	but the weather decided to break.
2 He lost his umbrella	b)	which proved to be tame.
3 He wore his best suit	c)	who couldn't stand men.
4 He trained as an actor	d)	the day of the rain.
5 He aimed for the yellow	e)	but landed a shark.
6 He worked very hard	f)	but nobody came.
7 He invested in shares	g)	while the others wore jeans.
8 He collected fine china	h)	but wounded a wren.

9 He bought a Picasso	i) which just wouldn't bark.
10 He stripped	j) but nobody went.
11 He held a big party	k) but was transferred to Spain
12 He hunted a tiger	l) until, sadly, he died.
13 He bought a huge watchdog	m) but all of it smashed.
14 He fished for a salmon	n) while the others all lied.
15 He played at roulette	o) but was given the sack.
16 He opened a cafe	p) which turned out a fake.
17 He shot at a pheasant	q) but potted the black.
18 He married a woman	r) but he lost every cent.
19 He stuck to the truth	s) then joined the marines.
20 And so it went on	t) then the stock market crashed.

'Stan felt sticky'

Task 46   Here is another poem in rhyming couplets. Match the endings to the beginnings of each line.

1 Stan felt sticky, so he	a) went to see a friend
2 Ruth felt like running, so she	b) sang a lively song
3 Henry felt hot, so he	c) ran off to the beach.
4 Willy felt like walking, so he	d) wandered down the path
5 Fanny felt frozen, so she	e) went and picked a peach
6 Sally felt like sailing, so she	f) tried to sing along
7 Sammy felt small, so he	g) tried to hire a boat.
8 Cindy felt like selling, so she	h) had a little snooze
9 Hannah felt hungry, so she	i) grew a little higher
10 Sammy felt like swimming, so he	j) went and sat down
11 Freddy felt funny, so he	k) drove into the town
12 Shirley felt like shopping, so she	l) played a lonely blues
13 Sandy felt sad, so she	m) had a cold bath
14 Sally felt like sleeping, so she	n) went and got a coat
15 Harry felt happy, so he	o) went and had a shower
16 Jacky felt like joining in, so	p) went and found a buyer
17 Laurie felt lonely, so she	q) jogged for half an hour

Benny went to bed, so that had better be the end.

'Mustn't grumble'

We British are known for our understatements. If you ask people from the USA how they are, they're likely to reply 'Fine!' , 'Great!' or 'Never been better!', all with firm falling tones. In Britain, you're more likely to hear 'Not too bad', or 'Could be worse', with that very British fall-rise. My two favourite replies are 'mustn't grumble' and 'can't complain'. And it was while thinking about how these normally involve both elision and assimilation – /ˈmʌsəŋ ˈɡrʌmbl/, /ˈkɑːŋ kəmˈpleɪn/ – that the idea for this poem came to me.

Task 47 Some of the words below are missing from the poem (a few extra words have been thrown in). As you can see, they all rhyme either with grumble or complain. Fill each gap in the poem with an appropriate word. You may use an English dictionary if you wish.

train	pain	stain	cane	grain	again
rain	lane	main	explain	chain	insane
rumble	tumble	humble	fumble	bumble	stumble
crumble (see c) below)			jumble (see d) below)		

Vocabulary notes

a) a *cockroach* is a dark-brown or black insect, sometimes found in kitchens;

b) the *naughty snowflakes* refer to one winter when trains in the south of England stopped running because, as British Rail explained, the snow was 'the wrong kind';

c) a *crumble* is a type of pudding, with a topping made of flour (or flour and muesli) mixed with brown sugar;

d) *jumble* is used in the sense of *jumble sale*, where people give away things (especially clothes) to be sold for charity.

'Mustn't grumble', 'Can't complain'
our traditional refrain.
Don't be pushy, best be humble.
Don't complain, and never grumble.

Broken pavings make you (1) ....?
Cockroach in your apple (2) ....?
Mustn't grumble, can't complain.

8:05 is late (3) ....?
Naughty snowflakes stopped the (4) ....?
Don't complain, you shouldn't grumble.

Government begins to (5) ....?
Housing prices start to (6) ....?
Mustn't grumble, can't complain.

Global warming brings more (7) ....
Medicine won't kill the (8) ....?
Don't complain, no need to grumble.

Kiddy's clothes come from the (9) ....?
Somewhere guns begin to (10) ....?
Do not ask them to (11) ....;
just accept it, don't complain.
Mustn't grumble,
Mustn't grumble,
Mustn't grumble.

'My mother said'

This is an old anonymous poem (that means we don't know who wrote it). As it gets near the end, and the speaker jumps on the horse, the number of unstressed syllables increases and you have to speak faster to keep to the beat of the horse's hooves.

My mother said, I never should
play with the gypsies in the wood.

If I did then she would say:
'Naughty child to disobey!'

'Your hair shan't curl and your shoes shan't shine,
You gypsy child, you shan't be mine!'

And my father said that if I did,
he'd rap my head with the teapot lid.

My mother said that I never should
play with the gypsies in the wood.

The wood was dark, the grass was green;
By came Sally with a tambourine.

I went to sea – no ship to get across;
I paid ten shillings for a blind white horse.

I upped on his back and was off in a crack,
Sally tell my mother I shall never come back.

'On your bike'

I really think I must be the only person in London who regularly rides a bike but can also drive a car. Car and lorry drivers have no idea of the space that cyclists need and are often a great danger to them; and cyclists fail to realize, for example, that motorists do not expect to be overtaken by a cyclist coming up between them and the pavement.

By the way, I do not recommend you to call people *idiots*, *bastards* or *berks* unless you want a fight.

A   When I'm on my bike I am the angel of the street;
I'm courteous and friendly to everyone I meet.

I never mount the pavement, I just keep to the road;
I don't infringe in any way the sacred Highway Code.

I signal to the motorists and make my movements clear;
I ride along the gutter and I never swerve or veer.

But what about those bastards in their lorries and their cars?
They stare at me suspiciously as if I came from Mars.

That's if they even notice me as zombie-like they drive;
I need my wits about me if I want to stay alive.

They pass and then turn left or open doors right in my face;
I sometimes think that drivers aren't aware we need some space.

So when you see me cycling in my helmet and my mask,
just use a little courtesy; is that too much to ask?

B   Now when I'm at the wheel I'm always perfectly polite;
aware of all the cyclists, sympathetic to their plight.

I follow very carefully the details of the Code;
I flash to let them cut across a really busy road;

I check the nearside mirror just in case there's one in sight;
and take especial care whenever driving late at night.

But what about those bastards cycling merrily along?
You'd think their parents never tried to teach them right from wrong.

They pass you on the left when you are checking to the right,
then wave their stupid fists at you; they do it out of spite.

They go both ways down one-way streets, turn left when lights are red.
The bloody little idiots deserve to end up dead!

So when you see me in my car while cycling to work,
just use some common sense, can't you, you stupid little berk!

When in my car or on my bike it's very plain to see;
the roads are full of lunatics,
with one exception:
ME!

Chapter 12
Similes, sayings and sounds

In this final part of the book we will play with the magic of words and rhythm, concentrating on words and phrases that belong so closely together that you have to learn the rhythm of the phrase together with its meaning.

Similes

If you say that something is *as light as a feather* or *as heavy as lead*, you are using a simile: comparing one thing with another.

Some similes are so common that they have become cliches, expressions you use without thinking about them. Others are more original and cause the listener to think in a new way about what you are referring to.

And some similes are so old that we understand them as a whole, but not the individual words. If, for example, you say that something is *as plain as a pikestaff*, we know that it means 'absolutely obvious; 100% clear', but hardly anybody knows what a *pikestaff* actually is. In fact, it was a smooth type of stick, and the simile originally meant 'as smooth as a pikestaff' (i.e., with no lumps, bumps or decorations).

This particular simile, together with several others, is found in the first poem in this section.

'As' (anonymous)

This is a poem made up entirely of well-known, proverbial similes. There is heavy stress on the adjectives and nouns, while the grammatical words *and* and *as* are very short, both containing schwa. When you repeat it, remember to make the links in, for example, wet‿as‿a / dry‿as‿a / poor‿as‿a / free‿as the‿air.

> **Vocabulary notes**
> *moles* are short-sighted animals which live underground. Their soft skin used to be made into clothes (especially mole-skin trousers);
> *partridges* are game birds, i.e., birds bred to be shot and eaten in the autumn. They are plump (= 'fat') because they are ready to eat;
> *a pikestaff* (now archaic) was a type of stick with a plain (= smooth) surface; nowadays, the expression as plain as a pikestaff = 'obvious, self-evident'.

As **wet** as a **fish** – as **dry** as a **bone**;
As **live** as a **bird** – as **dead** as a **stone**;
As **plump** as a **partridge** – as **poor** as a **rat**;
As **strong** as a **horse** – as **weak** as a **cat**;
As **hard** as **flint** – as **soft** as a **mole**;
As **white** as a **lily** – as **black** as **coal**;
As **plain** as a **pikestaff** – as **rough** as a **bear**;
As **tight** as a **drum** – as **free** as the **air**;
As **heavy** as **lead** – as **light** as a **feather**;
As **steady** as **time** – uncertain as **weather**

'Sensible similes'

Task 48 In this poem, the first line of each couplet is made up of two well-known similes. The second (rhyming) line has been made up by me. I call these 'sensible' similes, since they all make sense (compared to the 'silly similes' that follow). Your task is to put the following adjectives into the correct places in the poem. The first couplet is complete.

> **Vocabulary notes**
> *common* is used here in the sense of 'vulgar, badly educated, badly behaved';
> a *fiddle* is a violin (a stringed instrument), though why it should be associated with good health I do not know;
> *fit* in this sense means 'in good condition, in good health';
> *icing* is a sugary topping for cakes, especially for birthdays and Christmas;
> *keen* is used in the sense of 'eager, enthusiastic', though other meanings include 'sharp, acute, strong', as in the expression 'a keen sense of smell';
> *long locks* = 'long hair';
> a *peacock* is a male bird, with extremely beautiful tail feathers;
> a *rake* is a long garden instrument used to rake up (or remove by pulling along the ground) dead leaves, plants, etc.;
> a *rocker*, in this sense, is a rock musician, especially one who plays loud, older forms of rock music;
> a *tether* is a line or rope attaching an animal (horse, goat, dog, etc.) to a particular place. When it is *at the end of its tether* it can go no further, so this has come to mean 'frustrated, impatient, ready to crack up'.

tight	proud	steady	cool	thin	poor	sad
bold	keen	strange	fit	strong	blind	happy
wild	clever	deep	common	light	sickly	rough

As white as a lily, as blue as the sky,
as bright as the flags on the Fourth of July.

As (1) .... as a cucumber, (2) .... as a drum,
as (3) .... as a child falling flat on its bum.

As (4) .... as a bat, as (5) .... as a feather,
as (6) .... as a horse at the end of its tether.

As (7) .... as a church mouse, as (8) .... as muck,
as (9) .... as Chinese men dining on duck.

As (10) .... as a peacock, as (11) .... as brass,
as (12) .... as kids who are top of the class.

As (13) .... as mustard, as (14) .... as an ox,
as (15) .... as a rocker with long, filthy locks.

As (16) .... as a fiddle, as (17) .... as a rake,
as (18) .... as icing on top of a cake.

As (19) .... as the ocean, as (20) .... as time,
as (21) .... as a simile used in a rhyme.

'Silly similes'

The vocabulary in this poem is difficult, since these are really anti-similes: the adjectives have nothing at all to do with the nouns. In fact it is a nonsense poem, in the tradition of Lewis Carroll. If I were you, I wouldn't bother about the meaning at all to start with; just let the words roll over you.

> **Vocabulary notes**
> *blunt* is the opposite of sharp (as in a knife, razor, etc.);
> *cruel as a cucumber* is a variant of *cool as a cucumber* (= calm), which we met in 'Sensible similes';
> *Michaelmas Day* is the feast day of Saint Michael, my patron saint;
> *mildew* is a disease that affects plants;
> *mutton* is sheep-meat. (The meat from a young sheep is lamb.);
> a *rissole* is a type of meat dish;
> a *waistcoat* is what is worn under the jacket in a three-piece suit. In the USA, it is called a *vest*;
> you *weave* cloth, wool, silk, etc., not pies, of course.

As fond as a finger, as safe as a spoon,
as cruel as a cucumber planted in June.

As bold as a button, as mildewed as May,
as merry as mutton from foggy Bombay.

As fast as a feather, as grand as a glove,
as weary as weather all limpid with love.

As blunt as a blazer, as clever as clay,
as ripe as a razor on Michaelmas Day.

As high as a handle, as hot as a hare,
as scarce as a scandal in Washington Square.

As lean as a lever, as silken as sighs,
as wet as a weaver of marmalade pies.

As weak as a waistcoat, as fat as a flea,
as pale as a parson from sunny Dundee.

As proud as a plum stone, as poor as a peach,
as wise as a whistle on Cheltenham beach.

As tough as a tailor, as drunk as a door,
as soft as a sailor at quarter to four.

As rich as a rissole, as dense as a duck,
as sad as a simile down on its luck.

Sayings and proverbs

English, like all languages, has a large number of sayings and proverbs. And many of them are rhythmic and often contain alliteration and rhymes.

Task 49   Listen to the following and then match them with the explanations.

1 Their bark is worse than their bite.
2 A bird in the hand is worth two in the bush.
3 It's no use crying over spilt milk.
4 Too many cooks spoil the broth.
5 A stitch in time saves nine.
6 There's many a slip twixt (= between) cup and lip.
7 All that glitters is not gold.
8 Don't count your chickens before they're hatched.
9 Least said, soonest mended.
10 Easy come, easy go.

a) People with similar tastes and interests tend to meet up.
b) Remedy any slight defects early before things start to get really bad.
c) Unsupervised people are likely to misbehave.
d) It is best not to be too optimistic about the outcome of your projects.
e) Things acquired with little effort are likely to be just as easily lost.

11 Birds of a feather flock together.
12 To put the cart before the horse.
13 To put the cat among the pigeons.
14 When the cat's away the mice will play.
15 The pot calling the kettle black.
16 Two heads are better than one.
17 To make a mountain out of a molehill.
18 Don't put all your eggs in one basket.
19 Give them an inch, they'll take a mile.
20 Better be safe than sorry.

f) You are more likely to make the correct decision having asked for a second opinion.
g) To get your priorities wrong.
h) They are likely to take advantage if you make the slightest concession.
i) They sound more threatening than they actually are.
j) There is no point complaining about past events that cannot be changed.
k) To stir up trouble deliberately.
l) Pay more attention to what you have than to what you might possibly have.
m) Do not be fooled by outward appearances.
n) To make too much of something rather trivial.
o) Caution is often the best approach.
p) 'No comment' may well be the wisest choice.
q) It can be unwise to have too many people collaborating on a project.
r) Things can go wrong, even at the very last moment.
s) Accusing someone of a defect that you also have.
t) It's best not to pin your hopes on a single person or project.

Doubling up sounds

English is full of phrases in which sounds are doubled. This may involve:

alliteration   e.g., *spick and span / topsy turvey / head over heels*
rhyme   e.g., *doom and gloom / namby pamby / funny money*
vowel change alone   e.g., *mish mash / zig zag / criss cross / tittle tattle*

A surprising number of such phrases start with the letter *h* (corresponding to the sound /h/). Here is a selection of them.

Task 50 Listen to them, then see if you can match them with the definitions.

1 hale and hearty (*adj.*)
2 hanky panky (*noun*)
3 helter skelter (*adv.*)
4 higgledy piggledy (*adj./adv.*)
5 high and mighty (*adj.*)
6 hurly burly (*noun*)
7 hocus pocus (*noun*)
8 hoi polloi (*noun*)
9 head over heels (*adj.*)
10 huffing and puffing (*v.*)
11 (by) hook or by crook (*adv.*)
12 hooray Henry (*noun*)
13 hunky dory (*adj.*)
14 hugger mugger (*adj./adv./phr.*)
15 hot spot (*noun*)
16 hot pot (*noun*)
17 hotch potch (*noun*)
18 hoo-ha (*noun*)
19 humdrum (*adj.*)
20 hob-nob (*v.*)

a) (done) in a great and disorganised hurry
b) breathing noisily
c) any way possible, including dishonest means
d) noisy activity
e) in disorder; mixed together any old how
f) very healthy and active
g) cheating or deceit or sexually improper behaviour of a not very serious kind
h) fine, OK
i) noisy talk or fuss about something unimportant
j) disorder
k) too ordinary; without variety or change
l) a number of things mixed up without any sensible order or arrangement
m) too proud and certain of one's own importance
n) the ordinary people
o) a loud-mouthed, empty-headed, upper-class man
p) to have a pleasant social relationship, often with someone in a higher social position
q) a place where there is likely to be a lot of trouble
r) completely, uncontrollably
s) a mutton, potato and onion stew
t) the use of tricks to deceive

Rhymes and Rhythm

Task 51   Fill each gap in the following sentences with one of the phrases (1–20) from Task 50.

1 He's not very fit, poor man. He was .... just 10 minutes after the start of the match.
2 In cheap supermarkets, they often pile up things all .... instead of putting them neatly on the shelves.
3 He's gone all .... since he got that new job. Won't have anything to do with his old friends.
4 They hardly ever go out; never been abroad. A pretty .... life altogether, if you ask me.
5 I'll get my own back on them ....
6 I hear the vicar's been up to a bit of .... with someone in the choir!
7 They couldn't cope in the .... of life.
8 How's things? Everything ....?

Finally, to end the book, here are two nonsense sequences using a number of doubled-up phrases. Look up the meanings in a good dictionary, if you want to. But if I were you, I would just do as I have suggested before; enjoy the magic of sounds, and listen to the rhythm and music of the language.

149

hanky panky	tall and lanky
hale and hearty	arty farty
hubble bubble	toil and trouble
hurdy gurdy	rather wordy
hurly burly	short and curly
hocus pocus	out of focus
hunky dory	thirteenth story
helter skelter	gimme shelter

see saw	hee haw
knick knack	tick tack
mish mash	splish splash
flip flop	tip top
chitter chatter	pitter patter
ping pong	ding dong
hi-fi	bye bye

Appendices

Appendix 1
Key to the tasks

Part I: Syllables, stress and rhythm

Task 1, page 4

biology	(4)	bridge	(1)	strength	(1)	photographer	(4)
watches	(2)	unabridged	(3)	support	(2)	jumped	(1)
jumpers	(2)	policeman	(3)	decided	(3)	obeyed	(2)

Task 2, page 5

	1 syllable	2 syllables	3 syllables	4 syllables
Cities	Leith	Cardiff	Manchester	Wolverhampton
Boys' names	George	Peter	Anthony	Alexander
Girls' names	Ann	Janet	Jemima	Felicity
Animals	bear	giraffe	elephant	rhinoceros
Countries	Spain	Japan	Morocco	Afghanistan
Rivers	Nile	Volga	Amazon	Mississippi

Task 3, page 6

■ ○ ○	○ ■ ○	○ ○ ■
Manchester	Jemima	
Anthony	Morocco	
elephant		
Amazon		

Task 4, page 6

○ ■ ○ ○	○ ○ ■ ○
Felicity	Alexander
Afghanistan	Wolverhampton
rhinoceros	Mississippi

Task 5, page 8

grower	yellow	aloud	hunted	forgive	photo
Timothy	Germany	bananas	workmanship	tomorrow	Elizabeth
Argentina	photograph	photography	photographic		

> **Note:** *Elizabeth* can start with short /ɪ/ or with schwa. And do not worry about the change of stress and of vowels in *photograph, photographic* and *photography*. The stress pattern of these, and of other words, is rule-based, as we shall see.

92

Task 6, page 9

This is **the** house **that** Jack built.
/'ðɪs ɪz ðə 'haʊs ðət 'dʒæk 'bɪlt/

These **are the** houses **that** Jack built.
/'ðiːz ə ðə 'haʊsɪz ðət 'dʒæk 'bɪlt/

Those **are the** people we drove **to the** party.
/'ðəʊz ə ðə 'piːpəl wi 'drəʊv tə ðə 'pɑːti/

That is **the** gardener who works **for** my mother.
/'ðæt ɪz ðə 'gɑːdnə huː 'wɜːks fə maɪ 'mʌðə/

Andrew is taller **than** Peter **and** Thomas.
/'ændruːʷ ɪz 'tɔːlə ðən 'piːtər ən 'tɒməs/

Fancy a glass **of** Italian brandy?
/'fænsɪʲ ə'glɑːs əv ɪ'tæljən 'brændi/

Tom's not **as** tall **as the** rest **of the** family.
/'tɒmz nɒt əz 'tɔːl əz ðə 'rest ə(v) ðə 'fæməli/

What **an** amazingly lively production.
/'wɒt ən ə'meɪzɪŋli 'laɪvli prə'dʌkʃən/

Task 7, page 15

a)

■	○■	■○	○■○	●○■○
Spain	Madrid	Venice	Verona	Algeciras
France	Toulouse	Brussels	Granada	Casablanca
Cannes	Algiers	Lisbon	Pamplona	
Rome	Tangier	Brisbane	Morocco	
Sfax		Malta	Gibraltar	
		Tunis	Valetta	

b) The odd one out is Santander = ●○■

Task 8, page 18

The following place names always have schwa:

Ventnor   *Plymouth*   *Poland*
/'ventnə/   /'plɪməθ/   /'pəʊlənd/

Brighton is either /'braɪtən/ (with schwa) or /'braɪtn̩/, with /n/ as syllabic consonant.

The rest are pronounced as follows: *Stockport* = /'stɒkpɔːt/; *Stockholm* = /'stɒkhəʊm/; *Stansted* = /'stænsted/; *Soho* = /'səʊhəʊ/.

Task 9, page 18

The following definitely have schwa in the first syllable:

bananas   vanilla   salami   pastrami   confetti   spaghetti   professor   confessor   baloney
computer   commuter

The following have schwa in the second syllable, not the first.

sarsparilla = /ˌsɑːspəˈrɪlə/; macaroni = /ˌmækəˈrəʊni/

The following usually has schwa in the first syllable, though some people use /ɪ/:

pyjamas = /pəˈdʒɑːməz/ or /prˈdʒɑːməz/

The following usually have /ɪ/ in the first syllable, though some people use schwa:

relation   libretto   stiletto

Task 10, page 18

The ones ending in ~a, ~er and ~or:

banana(s)	pyjama(s)	vanilla	sarsparilla
professor	confessor	computer	commuter

Note that *people* and *steeple* may either end in /əl/ or with syllabic /l/.

Task 11, page 18

provide	supply	collect	promote	consult	confuse
/prəˈvaid/	/səˈplai/	/kəˈlekt/	/prəˈməʊt/	/kənˈsʌlt/	/kənˈfjuːz/

Reform and *secure* usually have /ɪ/ in the first syllable, though some people use schwa.

Task 12, page 21

1 e)	6 b)	11 d)	16 n)
2 i)	7 r)	12 g)	17 a)
3 m)	8 k)	13 s)	18 o)
4 l)	9 j)	14 p)	19 c)
5 h)	10 f)	15 t)	20 q)

> **Note:** the adjectives *artful, sly* and *tricky* are fairly close in meaning. Look them up in a very good monolingual dictionary.

Task 13, page 22

1 g)	7 w)	13 o)	19 l)
2 p)	8 s)	14 k)	20 v)
3 j)	9 b)	15 t)	21 c)
4 f)	10 d)	16 h)	22 n)
5 e)	11 a)	17 x)	23 u)
6 m)	12 q)	18 i)	24 r)

Part II: Stress in words and phrases

Task 14, page 24

1 surprise	2 develop	3 reload	4 introduce
collect	abolish	pre-set	contradict
defend	consider	defuse	overwhelm
prefer	surrender	co-chair	undertake
refuse	determine	pre-paint	interfere
remove	enliven	demist	understand

5 tremble	6 estimate	7 realize
wander	clarify	circularize
soften	substitute	apologize
damage	accelerate	monopolize
measure	occupy	sentimentalize
worry	identify	idolize

Task 15, page 25

1 g)	5 j)	9 c)	13 i)
2 p)	6 k)	10 n)	14 b)
3 a)	7 m)	11 o)	15 d)
4 e)	8 f)	12 h)	16 l)

Task 16, page 30

a) *Selector, diver, confessor, translator, leader* and *teacher* all derive from verbs and keep the stress of the original verb *(doctor, barrister, tailor* and *broker* do not derive from verbs).

b) *Airman*, like *chairman*, is a compound noun composed of two elements, with stress on the first element – see Chapter 4.

c) *Democrat, astronaut* and *cosmonaut* are all composed of two classical elements, with stress on first syllable – see Chapter 4.

d) *Musician*, like *physician* (and most words ending in *ian* or *ion*, has the stress falling on the syllable before the end – see Stress imposing suffixes, p. 33).

e) *Photographer, zoologist, geographer* and *philanthropist* all end with a ■○○ suffix and are derived from ~y nouns – see Stress imposing suffixes, p. 33).

f) *Idealist, loyalist* and *realist* all derive from adjectives, with no change of stress – see Stress imposing suffixes, p. 33), *(balloonist* derives from a noun, not an adjective).

g) *Neurotic* like *psychotic*, ends with a suffix that imposes stress on the preceding syllable – see Stress imposing suffixes, p. 33).

Odd ones out:

Hack (= insulting term for a journalist) is a monosyllable, and *poet* fits none of the categories.

Task 17, page 37

1 p)	8 b)	15 n)	22 u)
2 h)	9 c)	16 v)	23 o)
3 y)	10 g)	17 t)	24 f)
4 q)	11 j)	18 d)	25 l)
5 a)	12 r)	19 bb)	26 w)
6 s)	13 aa)	20 x)	27 m)
7 z)	14 e)	21 i)	28 k)

Rhymes and Rhythm

Task 18, page 39

Phrases

a cotton 'dress	= a dress which is made of cotton
rubber 'gloves	= gloves which are made of rubber
a meat 'pie	= a pie which is made of meat
an English 'teacher	= a teacher who is English
a black 'bird	= a bird which is black
that white 'house	= that house which is white
a moving 'train	= a train which is moving
the winning 'horse	= the horse which won the race

Compounds

a 'cotton factory	= a factory where cotton is made
a 'rubber plant	= a type of plant
a 'meat packer	= a packer of meat/person who packs meat
an 'English teacher	= a teacher of English/person who teaches English
a 'blackbird	= a type of bird
the 'White House	= a particular house where the US President lives
a 'moving van	= a van used for moving furniture, etc.
the 'winning post	= the post which shows where the race ends

Task 19, page 40

Compounds

earrings   tennis shoes   riding breeches   evening gown   handbag   overcoats   underwear

Phrases

cheapish dress   cotton skirt   leather belt   silken blouses   linen shirt   flashy scarf   summer blouses   winter hose   cashmere sweaters

Task 20, page 44

1 through – stopped – Vaughan – knives

2 hungry – leather – follow – Michael – Leicester

3 Peru – Iran – a few – police – defend – Macbeth

4 dead drunk – red hot – tired out – next year – buy now

5 somebody – Hungary – sympathy – Manchester – after it

6 tomato – Madonna – policeman – embargo – a big one – Trafalgar

7 to the school – for a while – as a rule

8 best results – half a pound – outer space – Charing Cross

9 photographic – institution – Speaker's Corner – inner circle – Nelson's Column – buy a new one – half a sandwich

10 give me a drink – Madam Tussaud's – Royal Exchange – buy us some food – go to the bank

11 biology – maternity – the last of them – conservative – a pound of it – Elizabeth

12 come to the disco – geriatrician – Kensington High Street – offer him money – try a banana – Buckingham Palace

13 biographical – Peter Davidson – disability

14 sending a telegram – autobiography – all of the elephants

Task 21, page 47

one-night stand	a long-haired drummer	a rock 'n' roll band
a four-hour show	a first-rate gig	a well-earned hand
a red-headed woman	high-heeled shoes	a bald-headed fellow
an unnamed fan	stone-cold sober	absolutely grand
instrumental numbers	rock 'n' roll licks	bass-drum pedal

Part III: Fast, natural speech

Task 22, page 50

In the fast version, the final consonant of the numeral or adjective disappeared: the /t/ in *first, next* and *last*; and the /d/ in *second* and *third*.

The firs(t) girl and the firs(t) boy

The secon(d) girl and the secon(d) boy

The thir(d) girl and the thir(d) boy

The nex(t) girl and the nex(t) boy

The las(t) girl and the las(t) boy

Task 23, page 50

The /n/ of *secon(d) girl* changes to /ŋ/ (the sound at the end of *thing, song*, etc.)

The /n/ of *secon(d) boy* changes to /m/.

The /d/ of *third girl* changes to /g/.

The /d/ of *third boy* changes to /b/.

Task 24, page 52

2 a perfec(t) morning

3 perfec(t)ly marvellous

5 she wan(t)s ten poun(d)s of butter

6 he fin(d)s it boring

7 have the fac(t)s as soon as possible

8 I watch(ed) four differen(t) programmes las(t) night

9 Jane hates fas(t) food so she won('t) want any burgers

10 We're having roas(t) beef with bake(d) potatoes an(d) beans

Task 25, page 53

Elision of /d/ or /t/ is not possible in:

* *hardware, word processor* and *smart card*; *r* is not a spoken consonant, so /d/ and /t/ follow a vowel sound.
* *loud speaker* /d/ follows a vowel sound
* *turned off* /d/ is followed by a vowel sound
* Note that the /d/ of *word processor* and the /t/ of *smart card* may both change (i.e., may be assimilated).

Rhymes and Rhythm

Task 26, page 56

2 glad / sad / mad / bad

3 well / swell (you can look like hell = 'in a bad way').

4 glum (= 'sad') / numb (= unable to feel, from shock, etc.)

5 fat (a person can't be flat)

6 sick (you can't look quick; a person can look thick = 'appear stupid', but that means permanently)

7 smart

8 shy / sly (possibly high, too = 'under the influence of drugs')

9 slim / grim (= angry, in a bad mood)

10 thin

11 great

12 fine

13 blue (= sad)

Task 27, page 57

When /n/ does not change

The sound /n/ is an alveolar nasal, i.e., a nasal produced with the tongue touching the tooth ridge. If the next sound is also produced with the tongue in the same general area, then the transition from one sound to the next is easy. This is the case when /n/ is followed by /d/, /t/, /s/, /ʃ/, /θ/, /r/ and /l/, which explains why *ten* does not change in such contexts as: *ten dogs, ten downs, ten truths, ten sighs, ten saucers, ten shouts, ten things, ten rings, ten lies.*

When /n/ can change

1 /n/ can become the bilabial nasal /m/ before any other bilabials (i.e., sounds that involve closing of the lips):
   • before /b/ *ten brooches*;
   • before /p/ *ten parks, ten peaches, ten pearls*;
   • before /m/ *ten moons, ten monkeys*;
   • before /w/ *ten whales.*

2 /n/ can become the velar nasal /ŋ/ before the other two velar sounds (i.e., those where the back of the tongue touches the velum, or soft palate).
   • before /g/ *ten girls, ten gardens, ten grapes*;
   • before /k/ *ten cats, ten coats, ten cups.*

Task 28, page 59

Old Street	elision of /d/	/ˈəʊl ˌstriːt/
Holland Park	elision of /d/; /n/ becomes /m/	/ˌhɒləm ˈpɑːk/
Hyde Park	/d/ becomes /b/	/ˌhaɪb ˈpɑːk/
Old Kent Road	elision of /d/; /t/ becomes a glottal stop	/ˌəʊl ˌkenʔ ˈrəʊd/
Covent Garden	elision of /t/; /n/ becomes /ŋ/	/ˌkɒvəŋ ˈgɑːdən/
Bond Street	elision of /d/	/ˈbɒn ˌstriːt/
Saint Paul's	elision of /t/; /n/ becomes /m/	/ˌsəm ˈpɔːlz/
London Bridge	/n/ becomes /m/	/ˌlʌndəm ˈbrɪdʒ/

Task 29, page 60

on hands and knees   faster than walking   on one foot   no sense of hurry   usually in the country out of control

	on hands and knees	faster than walking	on one foot	no sense of hurry	usually in the country	out of control
jog		✓				
stroll				✓		
ramble					✓	
saunter				✓		
run		✓				
lurch						✓
crawl	✓					
hop			✓			
hike					✓	

Task 30, page 61

1 Southern fried chicken (note the elided /d/, *fried* sounds like *fry*)
2 ham and lettuce salad (the /s/ at the end of lettuce becomes part of the /s/ in *salad*. This means it sounds like *ham and letter salad*)
3 thousand island dressing (you hear the /d/ in *thousand* but not in *island*)
4 blue cheese
5 double western omelette (the /n/ of *western* links to *omelette*)
6 sausages
7 peas (*and peas* = /əm ˈpiːz/)
8 rack (= the ribs are not cut off and served individually)
9 ribs (= pork spare ribs)
10 barbecue sauce
11 king-size burger (= very large hamburger)
12 ketchup (a thick, sweet tomato sauce) (the /p/ links to *of*)
13 burger (the /r/ links to *in*)
14 sesame bun (a bun containing sesame seeds)
15 rump steak
16 onions
17 chilli (there's a /j/ link in *chilli on*)
18 steak and mushroom (*and mushroom* = /ə ˈmʌʃruːm/)
19 mashed potato (the /d/ is elided, so *mashed* sounds like *mash*)
20 French fries (usually called *chips* in Britain)
21 salt-beef sandwich (the /t/ of *salt* becomes a glottal stop)
22 French mustard
23 apple pie
24 scoops (the ice cream is scooped out with a special instrument)
25 ice cream (the linking makes it sound like *I scream*)
26 stack (= a little pile)
27 pancakes (assimilation makes it sound like *pang cakes*)

28 syrup (the /p/ links to *on*)
29 ice cream sundae (a rich mixture of ice cream, fruit, syrup, etc.)
30 cheesecake
31 strawberry
32 diet coke (the /t/ becomes a glottal stop. Note that coke is a registered trade mark of the Coca-Cola company)

Task 31, page 62

elision

bes(t) friend   bran(d) new   secon(d)-hand   nex(t)-door   lan(d)lord
poun(d)s   lan(d)lady   Chris(t)mas   las(t) week   promise(d) that   nex(t) week

elision and possible assimilation

san(d)wiches = *sanwiches* or *samwiches*

Task 32, page 62

elision giving rise to assimilation

han(d) bag = *hambag*   frien(d) bought = *frem bought*   han(d) mack = *ham mack*
len(d) me = *lem me*   corn(ed) beef = *corm beef*   gran(d)mother = *gram mother*
cann(ed) potatoes = *cam potatoes*

assimilation

made me = *mabe me*   at Christmas = /ək krɪsməs/

assimilation or glottal stop

a fortnigh(t) back = *a fortnipe back* or /fɔ?naɪ? bæk/
ge(t) my bags packed = *gep my* or /gə? maɪ/

/t/ = glottal stop

right now   bought me   brought me

coalescent assimilation

might use = *my choose* /maɪ tʃuːz/

Task 33, page 68

	/ʃ/	/ʒ/		/ʃ/	/ʒ/
course	✓		please		✓
discuss	✓		express	✓	
miss	✓		revise		✓
use		✓	pass	✓	
practise	✓		amaze		✓

Of course, it was those ending with /s/ which coalesced with /j/ to become /ʃ/, and those ending in /z/ which coalesced with /j/ to become /ʒ/.

Task 34, page 69

a) every example of **linking** in Verse 2

And words go together like‿links‿in‿a chain;
they follow‿each‿other like wagons‿on‿a train

consonant to vowel links: links‿in   in‿a   follow‿each   each‿other
wagons‿on   on‿a

consonant to consonant link: like‿links (sounds like *lie clinks*)

b) every example of **elision** in the introduction and Verse **5**.

If you wan(t) to make your English come alive, jus(t) listen to my rules from one to five.
You're getting better now, but to be the bes(t), jus(t) remember two soun(d)s can coalesce.

between two consonants: jus(t) listen jus(t) remember soun(d)s

identical sounds meeting: wan(t) to

similar sounds meeting + /t/ between two consonants: bes(t) just

c) every example of **anticipatory assimilation** in Verses **3,4** and **5**.

Now listen really close and you will hear
that certai**n k**inds of soun(**d**) **c**an disappear.

And remember if you want to increase your range
that a sou**n**(**d**) **c**an **m**ake another sound change.

You're getting better now, but to be the best,
just remember two sounds ca**n c**oalesce.

straight assimilation: certain kinds / can coalesce = /n/ → /ŋ/; can make = /n/ → /m/;

assimilation following /d/ elision: soun(d) can = /n/ → /ŋ/

d) every example of **coalescent assimilation** in the whole rap.

If you don(t) want your English
/ɪf jʊ ˈdəʊn ˈwʌntʃə ˈrɪŋglɪʃ/

But you're going to soun(d) funny,
/bʌtʃə ˈgəʊnə ˈsaʊn ˈfʌni/

Now listen really close and you will hear
/naʊ ˈlɪsn ˈrɪəli ˈkləʊs ən ˈdʒuː wɪl hɪə/

And remember if you want to increase your range
/ən rɪˈmembərɪf jə wʌn tʊ ʷɪŋ ˈkriːʃɔː ˈreindʒ/

/t/ + /j/ → /tʃ/: want your   but your

/d/ + /j/ → /dʒ/: and you

/s/ + /j/ → /ʃ/: increase your

Part IV: Playing with poems

Task 35, page 72

1 Crewe   3 night   5 true

2 shoe   4 fright

Task 36, page 73

1 Kong   4 note   7 bell   10 tell

2 song   5 gong   8 averred

3 wrote 6 Estelle 9 heard

Task 37, page 73

1 Crewe 4 about   7 dine   10 nine   13 suppose

2 stew   5 too   8 eleven 11 Kent   14 nose

3 shout 6 Rhine   9 seven   12 bent   15 went

Rhymes and Rhythm

Task 38, page 74

1 There was a young girl in the choir
2 Whose voice rose up higher and higher
3 Till it reached such a height
4 It was clear out of sight
5 And they found it next day in the spire.

6 A girl who weighed many an ounce
7 Used language I dare not pronounce.
8 For a fellow, unkind,
9 Pulled her chair out behind
10 Just to see (so he said) if she'd bounce.

11 A certain old lady from Crewe
12 Once dropped her false teeth in the stew.
13 Said a sensitive waiter
14 'It's horrid to cater
15 For careless old people like you!'

Task 39, page 74

1 **A sprightly old man from LA**
2 Once said to his wife, 'If I may
3 I think I will stand
4 **on my head in the Strand,'**
5 To which she retorted: 'okay.'

6 **A greedy old grandad from Duns,**
7 Once said he'd eat ninety-nine buns.
8 At the seventy-first,
9 **He unluckily burst,**
10 So the rest were consumed by his sons.

Task 40, page 74

There was an old man of Khartoum
Who kept two tame sheep in his room.
To remind him, he said
Of two friends who were dead;
But he could not remember of whom.

A greedy young lady called Perkins
Was awfully fond of small gherkins.
She devoured forty-three
One day for her tea
And pickled her internal workings.

When the shortage of fuel made it hard,
To maintain the big blaze in our yard;
We threw on Aunt Flo,
Who heightened the glow,
But I fear she became somewhat charred.

Task 41, page 79

(If more than one answer is possible, the first listed below is the original.)

1 down
2 town
3 jump / wave / clap
4 shout
5 money
6 each (*every* fits the meaning but is too long; *all* fits the metre but not the meaning)
7 spaghetti (you can't eat *confetti*)
8 sack / bag / pound
9 tin / can / bit / pound / sack / bag
10 cat

Task 42, page 79

(If more than one answer is possible, the first listed below is the original.)

11 beans
12 Peter
13 chocolate / sugar / biscuits
14 cake
15 pound
16 cheese
17 who / they
18 crates / pounds / bags
19 does / can
20 meat
21 time
22 heating

Tasks 43 and 44, page 81

(If more than one answer is possible, the first listed below is the original.)

1 tubes / trains (*buses* is too long)
2 buses
3 by / at / for
4 leave at eight
5 shining / rising / setting
6 gold
7 arrows / rainbows
8 glad / pleased (*happy* is too long)
9 explain
10/11 fumes, dirt, rain (other words such as *crowds, smog, filth*, etc., could also fit. If you put *fog*, then you have seen too many old Sherlock Holmes films!)
12 lorries / buses (*cars* is too short)
13 cycle (no, I don't *drive*, and the word's too short anyway)
14 nightfall / midnight
15 afraid (*frightened* is stressed on the wrong syllable. and *scared* is too short).
16 know (you *speak to* your neighbours)
17 after
18 use (you *look through* a hole)
19 at the door
20 concert
21 play / film
22 tell you why
23 die
24 dogs
25 dark
26 rubbish
27 pollution
28 breathing / sleeping?
29 seems to care
30 stroll/ walk
31/32 get ... down
33 agree
34 though / but
35 tired of life

Task 45, page 82

1 k)	4 s)	7 t)	10 a)	13 i)	16 j)	19 n)
2 d)	5 q)	8 m)	11 f)	14 e)	17 h)	20 l)
3 g)	6 o)	9 p)	12 b)	15 r)	18 c)	

Rhymes and Rhythm

Task 46, page 83

1 o)	4 d)	7 i)	10 c)	13 l)	16 f)
2 q)	5 n)	8 p)	11 j)	14 h)	17 a)
3 m)	6 g)	9 e)	12 k)	15 b)	

Task 47, page 84

1 stumble	4 train	7 rain	10 rumble
2 crumble	5 fumble	8 pain	11 explain
3 again	6 tumble	9 jumble	

Task 48, page 87

1 cool	4 blind	7 poor	10 proud	13 keen	16 fit	19 deep
2 tight	5 light	8 common	11 bold	14 strong	17 thin	20 steady
3 sad	6 wild	9 happy	12 clever	15 rough	18 sickly	21 strange

Task 49, page 88

1 i)	4 q)	7 m)	10 e)	13 k)	16 f)	19 h)
2 l)	5 b)	8 d)	11 a)	14 c)	17 n)	20 o)
3 j)	6 r)	9 p)	12 g)	15 s)	18 t)	

Task 50, page 89

1 f)	4 e)	7 t)	10 b)	13 h)	16 s)	19 k)
2 g)	5 m)	8 n)	11 c)	14 j)	17 l)	20 p)
3 a)	6 d)	9 r)*	12 o)	15 q)	18 i)	

*(in the expression *head over heels in love*)

Task 51, page 90

1 huffing and puffing

2 higgledy-piggledy

3 high and mighty

4 humdrum

5 by hook or by crook

6 hanky panky

7 hurly burly

8 hunky dory

Appendix 2
Completed poems

An acrobat is agile

An **ac**robat is agile and can somersault and leap;
An **oc**topus is something you might see beneath the deep.

A **ther**mostat is useful to control the rate of heat;
A **met**ronome is what you need to help you keep the beat

A **per**iscope is useful if you're in a submarine
A **chro**mosome is found in living cells, just like a gene.

A **ho**mophone's a word that sounds exactly like another;
A **tele**gram is something that you might send to your mother.

A **po**lymorph is something that can take on many shapes;
The **an**thropoids are shaped like us: the monkeys and the apes.

A **tele**phone's for talking to a person far away.
A **mi**crophone can pick up every single word you say.

A **hy**drofoil's a type of boat that skims across the sea;
A **pe**dagogue will teach your little children, for a fee.

A **cos**monaut might visit Venus, Jupiter or Mars;
An **as**tronaut could go much farther, even to the stars.

A **ger**micide is what can help to keep disease at bay;
A **disco**theque's for people who like dancing every day.

A **pho**tograph is known to certain people as a 'snap';
A **hyp**notist is someone who could help you take a nap.

A **po**lyglot might understand both Japanese and Czech;
A **ba**thysphere is useful if you want to see a wreck.

The **di**nosaurs all died out 60 millions years ago,
while **hy**drogen and **ox**ygen combine as H_2O.

An **aqua**duct is what will bring you water from afar;
A **via**duct, by contrast, is more useful for your car.

An **au**tograph is written with a pencil or a pen;
A **mo**nocle's occasionally worn by certain men.

A **po**lygraph is something you can use to trap a liar;
and **ae**rosols are things you shouldn't throw into a fire.

A **reg**icide is someone was has killed a king or queen
(A **mon**archist would never even dream of such a thing).

And if this kind of **lex**icon is hard to comprehend,
then you had better try to get a teacher as a friend.

(See Task 17, page 37.)

Rhymes and Rhythm

Down the diner

I was sitting down the diner, toying with my food,
looking at the papers, in a lazy kind of mood

when a little skinny fellow I'd never seen before
came and sat down beside me, and this is what I saw:

my favourite waitress, Sally, came over to the guy
to ask him for his order, and this was his reply:

'I'd like a southern fried chicken, make sure it's really hot,
and a ham and lettuce salad should really hit the spot,

with a thousand island dressing and a touch of blue cheese
then a double western omelette with some sausages and peas,

and a rack or two of ribs with some barbecue sauce
then a king-size burger, with some ketchup, of course.

Can I have the burger in a sesame bun?
and a good thick rump steak ... well-done;

and how about some onions, I like them lightly fried,
with a little piccalilli and some chilli on the side

and I'd like to try a couple of your steak and mushroom pies
with a pile of mashed potato and a plate of french fries

then a salt-beef sandwich – cut it really thick,
with a little French mustard, now that should do the trick.

For dessert I think I'll start with a good old apple pie
with several scoops of ice cream, pile' em really high;

then a stack of little pancakes with some syrup on top
and an ice cream sundae; perhaps I'd better stop.

No, maybe there's some cheesecake that you can recommend?
OK I'll take the strawberry and that'll be the end.'

So Sally took the order though she thought it was a joke,
then the fellow called her back and said,

'I'd like ... a diet coke.'

(See Task 30, page 61.)

Song for London

A The roads are full of potholes
and the streets are full of trash,
the pavements lined with youngsters
asking, 'can you spare some cash?'

The tubes are packed to bursting
and the buses always late.
If you want to get to town by noon
you'd better leave at eight.

But when the sun is shining
and the river glints like gold,
and the bridges curve like arrows,
then the city takes its hold.

And I'm glad to be in London,
though I really can't explain.
And London's where I live
despite the fumes, the dirt and rain.

B The lorries hurtle past me
as I cycle to my work.
If I come home after nightfall
I'm afraid of who might lurk.

You hardly know your neighbours
after 20 years or more,
and use a little spy hole
when someone's at the door.

But when I'm sitting waiting
for the concert to begin,
or a play by some young writer
makes me think that we might win,

then I'm glad to be in London,
though it's hard to tell you why.
And London is the city
where I'll live until I die.

C The dogs mess up the pavement,
the kids daren't use the park;
the traffic wrecks the daytime;
alarms disturb the dark.

The rubbish chokes the gutters,
pollution fills the air,
old folks have trouble breathing
and no-one seems to care.

But when I stroll at weekends
through Brick Lane or Camden Town,
I realize that, though
there's plenty here to get me down,

I agree with Doctor Johnson
(though I can't speak for my wife)
that a man who's tired of London
is a man who's tired of life.

(See Tasks 43 and 44, pages 81–82.)

Stan felt sticky

Stan felt sticky, so he went and had a shower;
Ruth felt like running, so she jogged for half an hour.

Henry felt hot, so he had a cold bath;
Willy felt like walking, so he wandered down the path.

Fanny felt frozen, so she went and got a coat;
Sally felt like sailing, so she tried to hire a boat.

Sammy felt small, so he grew a little higher;
Cindy felt like selling, so she went and found a buyer.

Hannah felt hungry, so she went and picked a peach;
Sammy felt like swimming, so he ran off to the beach.

Freddy felt funny, so he went and sat down;
Shirley felt like shopping, so she drove into the town.

Sandy felt sad, so she played a lonely blues;
Sally felt like sleeping, so she had a little snooze.

Harry felt happy, so he sang a lively song;
Jacky felt like joining in, so tried to sing along.

Laurie felt lonely, so she went to see a friend;

Benny went to bed, so that had better be the end.

(See Task 46, page 83.)

Mustn't grumble

'Mustn't grumble', 'Can't complain':
our traditional refrain.
Don't be pushy, best be humble.
Don't complain, and never grumble.

Broken pavings make you stumble?
Cockroach in your apple crumble?
Mustn't grumble, can't complain.

8:05 is late again?
Naughty snowflakes stopped the train?
Don't complain, you shouldn't grumble.

Government begins to fumble?
Housing prices start to tumble?
Mustn't grumble, can't complain.

Global warming brings more rain?
Medicine won't kill the pain?
Don't complain, no need to grumble.

Kiddy's clothes come from the jumble?
Somewhere guns begin to rumble?
Do not ask them to explain;
just accept it, don't complain.
Mustn't grumble,
Mustn't grumble,
Mustn't grumble,

(See Task 47, page 84.)

Sensible similes

As white as a lily, as blue as the sky,
as bright as the flags on the Fourth of July.

As cool as a cucumber, tight as a drum,
as sad as a child falling flat on its bum.

As blind as a bat, as light as a feather,
as wild as a horse at the end of its tether.

As poor as a church mouse, as common as muck,
as happy as Chinese men dining on duck.

As proud as a peacock, as bold as brass,
as clever as kids who are top of the class.

As keen as mustard, as strong as an ox,
as rough as a rocker with long, filthy locks.

As fit as a fiddle, as thin as a rake,
as sickly as icing on top of a cake.

As deep as the ocean, as steady as time,
as strange as a simile used in a rhyme.

(See Task 48, page 87.)

Pages	Name	Pronunciation	Topics/vocabulary	Grammar
13	Billy yate a napple	Four ways to link words	Different types of food, and matchig adjectives, e.g., *juicy + orange*	*X ate a(n) Y*
14–15	And what kind of summer did **you** have?	Stressed and weak syllables/linking/stress pattern of place names	Travelling through Europe and North Africa	Range of verbs in past simple: *drove / spoke / gave / stayed / sailed /* etc.
15–16	Names	Front stress in names ■○(○): weak final syllables in place names / alliteration	First names and place names: *Norman + Nottingham, Mary + Marlow,* etc.	*X is from Y / X's from Y*
16–18	Where do you think you're going?	Stress in words ending in *a, o, i* / alliteration	Range of verbs + nouns: *Sell some salami / buy some bananas,* etc.	*Going to + verb phrase*
18	**Kenneth** bought some **cabbage**	Two-part alliteration	Range of thinks to eat or drink	*X bought some Y*
19	**Kenneth** bought a **kilo** of **cabbage**	Three-part alliteration	Containers, weights, etc.: *kilo / pound / tin / bunch / slice,* etc.	*X bought a(n) X of Y*
19	**Arthur** bought an **armful** of **artichokes**	Three-part alliteration (in poem) plus one example of vowel repetitio	More containers, weights, etc.	*X bought a(n) X of Y*
20	**Kenneth collected** a **kilo** of **cabbage**	Four-part alliteration	Variety of verbs replacing *bought. Collected / purchased / delivered,* etc.	*X verb + ed a(n) X of Y*
20–21	**Artful Arthur argued** for an **armful** of **artichokes**	Five-part (or six-part) alliteration	Variety of adjectives to modify the subjects and objects. *Beautiful / brash / careful / cheerful / clever / dirty,* etc.	*Adjective X verb + ed a(n) X of Y*
26–27	Percy = ■○ perSuade = ○■	Front stress in two-syllable nouns = ■○ End stress in two-syllable verbs = ○■	Range of verbs. The task is to find which nouns, verbs, etc., go (i.e., collocate) with them	*persuade* + someone to do s'thing; *behave* + adverb; *decide* + to do s'thing; *escape* + from s'one / s'thing / etc.
30–31	Who's who?	Stress pattern of longer nouns, including compounds	Nouns derived from verbs, nouns and adjectives: *collect/collector; magic/magician; photograph/ photographer; balloon/balloonist; real/realist,* etc.	Relative clauses such as: *a cosmonaut, circling the moor; a chairman who can't tell a lie; a wrestler whose job gets him down*
37–38	An acrobat	Compound nouns containing elements from Latin and Greek: e.g. Telephone = ■○○	The meaning of elements such as: *tele / phone / peri / glot / chrom / morph / aqua / scope / via*	
40–41	A cautionary tale	Compound names (with front stress) and phrases (with late stress)	Shopping for women's clothes and the danger of using credit cards too freely	
46	A **first**-class ticket, to travel first-**class**	Stress shift according to function and position		Compound adjectival phrases: *rent-free / first-class / outdoor /* etc.

Pages	Name	Pronunciation	Topics/vocabulary	Grammar
47–48	A long-haired drummer	More about stress shift.	Playing in a rock 'n' roll band	
51	The first girl said.	When sounds disappear (= elision); /d/ and /t/	Words to do with cooking and speaking	
55–56	Have you seen Peter? (1)	Weak forms of 'her', 'him' and 'them'		I *saw* him (or) I've *seen* him (running down the street / strolling in the park / walking up the hill / etc.)
56	Have you seen Peter? (2)	Weak forms of 'her', 'him' and 'them'	Range of adjectives describing people's appearance: neat / sweet / blue / numb / grim / thin / sick / glum / sad / great / smart / etc.	I *saw* him (or) I've *seen* him looking very / rather / really + adjective
57	Ten boys and ten girls	How sounds can change (= assimilation): Tem boys and teng girls		
59–60	Born and bred in London	Elision and assimilation in place names. Green Park → Greem Park; Old Street → Ole Street	Places in London Verbs of movement: jog / stroll / ramble / saunter / run / lurch / crawl / hop / hike	
61	Down the diner	Elision and assimilation in fast speech	Ordering food in an American restaurant: Southern fried chicken / ham and lettuce salad / steak and mushroom pies / thousand island dressing / etc.	Polite ordering: I'd like … / I think I'll start with … / How about … / OK I'll take the … / Can I have … /
62	Cash flow problems	Elision and assimilation in fast speech	Borrowing things and owing money Slang words	
66–67	Chinatown	How two words can join together (= coalescent assimilation) especially in very fast speech	Making arrangements: Where do you want to go → where dja wanna go? What do you recommend → watcha recommend? etc.	Fast forms of do you / don't you / would you / could you / couldn't you / where do you / what do you / did you / won't you / where would you / how did you / etc.
68–69	Rapping the rules	Summary of what happens in fast speech	How to sound like a native speaker (if that's what you want to do)	
76–77	So you think you've got problems?	Poem entirely in limericks	Pronunciation problems of various learners	
79–80	Going shopping	Listening out for rhymes, and words which have the right syllables and stress pattern to fit the gaps	Shopping for food and drink: Bread / jam / honey / wine / beer / stout / spaghetti / mutton chops / macaroni / baloney / artichokes / beans / etc.	

Pages	Name	Pronunciation	Topics/vocabulary	Grammar
80	Song for London	Listening out for rhymes, and words which have the right syllables and stress pattern to fit the gaps	Advantages and disadvantages of living in a big city	*If X happens …* / *but Y happens …*
82–83	Failure	Matching rhymed lines correctly	Story of a man with good intentions, but everything goes wrong	Matching main clause to the correct relative or subordinate clause
83	Stan felt sticky	Alliteration of name and adjective	Adjectives such as *hot* / *frozen* / *funny* / *sad* / *happy* / *lonely* / etc.	a) *feel + adjective* b) *feel like + Ving*
84	Mustn't grumble	Poem with only two rhymes, for ***grumble*** and com***plain***	How the British (the English especially) accept things without complaining	
85	On your bike		Getting around the city from the point of view of cyclists and motorists	
86–87	As / sensible similes		Accepted collocations: *As heavy as lead* / *as white as a lily* / etc.	
88	Silly similes		Unexpected collocations	
88–89	Sayings and proverbs		Matching common proverbs with their modern meaning	

Appendix 4
CD-ROM thumbnails

Here a sample of the supporting visuals available on the CD-ROM. You could use these on an overhead projector, interactive whiteboard or as handouts.

Visual 3

■   ■   ■

Jane,	Susan an(d)	Timothy.
Susan,	Jane an(d)	Timothy.
Timothy,	Jane an(d)	Susan.
Timothy,	Susan an(d)	Jane.
Jane,	Timothy an(d)	Susan.
Susan,	Timothy an(d)	Jane.
Sue,	Tim an(d)	Jane.
Jane,	Tim an(d)	Sue.
Tim,	Sue an(d)	Jane.

Visual 5(c)

■○○

Lewisham	'luː ɪ ʃəm
Westminster	'westmɪn stə
Paddington	'pæd ɪŋ tən
Farringdon	'fæ rɪŋ dən
Wimbledon	'wɪm bəldən
Tottenham	'tɒ tə nəm
Mornington	'mɔː nɪŋ tən
Shaftesbury	'ʃɑːfts bə ri
Barbican	'bɑː bɪ kən

Visual 7(a)

		man	go
		tan	go
		vi	sa
		da	ta
	ba	na	na
	lam	ba	da
	po	ta	to
	so	pra	no
a	vo	ca	do
pa	so	do	ble
Ca	li	for	nia
ka	ra	o	ke

Visual 7(b)

•	○	■	○
		man	go
		tan	go
		vi	sa
		da	ta
	ba	na	na
	lam	ba	da
	po	ta	to
	so	pra	no
a	vo	ca	do
pa	so	do	ble
Ca	li	for	nia
ka	ra	o	ke

Visual 11(a)

■○   ○■(○)

Percy	persuade
Betty	become
Dennis	develop
Annie	announce
Colin	collect
Connie	conduct
Desmond	devote
Debbie	decide
Oscar	object
Susie	suggest
Bennie	behave
Rita	record

Visual 13(a)

○	■	(○)
co	llect	
co	llect	or
com	pute	
com	put	er
a	llow	
a	llow	ance
a	ccount	
a	ccount	ant
en	quire	
en	quir	y
e	quip	
e	quip	ment

Visual 14

(○)■○   →   (○)■○○

manage	management
manage	manager
censor	censorship
credit	creditor
edit	editor
settle	settlement
accomplish	accomplishment
develop	development

Visual 15

Final /n/ and /l/

listen	middle
often	pedal
reason	little
certain	medal
sudden	saddle
pattern	needle
condition	vertical
collision	musical
profession	spherical

Visual 18

↘ book	lover
↘ book	shop
↘ meeting	room
↘ class	room
↘ foot	ball
↘ football	player
↘ shopping	basket
↘ walking	stick
↘ hand	bag
↘ English	teacher

Notes